Horse *Miracles*

Inspirational True Stories
of Remarkable Horses

Brad Steiger &
Sherry Hansen Steiger

Avon, Massachusetts

Published by
Adams Media, a division of F+W Media, Inc.
57 Littlefield Street, Avon, MA 02322 U.S.A.
www.adamsmedia.com and *www.cupofcomfort.com*

ISBN-10: 1-60550-019-4
ISBN-13: 978-1-60550-019-5
Printed in the United States of America.

J I H G F E D

Library of Congress Cataloging-in-Publication Data
available from publisher.

Interior photo © istockphoto.com

Previously published as *Horse Miracles*, by Brad Steiger and Sherry Hansen
Steiger, copyright © 2004 by Brad Steiger and Sherry Hansen Steiger,
ISBN-10: 1-59337-023-7, ISBN-13: 978-1-59337-023-7.

This publication is designed to provide accurate and authoritative information with
regard to the subject matter covered. It is sold with the understanding that the publisher
is not engaged in rendering legal, accounting, or other professional advice. If legal advice
or other expert assistance is required, the services of a competent professional person
should be sought.
—From a *Declaration of Principles* jointly adopted by a Committee of the
American Bar Association and a Committee of Publishers and Associations

Many of the designations used by manufacturers and sellers to distinguish their prod-
ucts are claimed as trademarks. Where those designations appear in this book and
Adams Media was aware of a trademark claim, the designations have been printed
with initial capital letters.

While all the events and experiences recounted in this book are true and happened
to real people, some of the names, dates, and places have been changed in order to
protect the privacy of certain individuals.

This book is available at quantity discounts for bulk purchases.
For information, please call 1-800-289-0963.

Foreword

Around 10,000 years ago, an early equine species vanished completely from the North American continent, and in many of the ancient civilizations in Africa, Asia, and Europe, humans didn't quite know what to do with horses. Then, around 3,000 years ago, horses were domesticated in Europe for the first time and were used for the transportation of both humans and trade goods.

Once the utilitarian problem of what to do with horses was solved, it didn't take long for the animal to achieve a divine or semi-divine status. In ancient Babylon, the horse was identified with the god Zu. The Greek word for horse is *ikkos*, the "great light," and the Greeks placed Pallas Athena, their goddess of wisdom, in a chariot drawn by four fiery horses. The great Greek philosopher Plato stated that the horse at its best signified reason coursing through the natural flow of things, and at its worst represented fantasy.

The Hebrew word for horse means "to explain," thus equating the animal with the human intellect. The Latin *equus* resolves into the light of the great mind or soul. In old France, a flower-laden horse served as the symbol for the Divine Mind and Reason in various ceremonies. The traditional nursery rhyme that tells of a White Lady who rides a white horse and whose bells make music wherever she goes is quite likely referring to our Lady of Wisdom.

To the ancient Vikings, the god Odin rode a swift horse across the sky and down into the realm of death. Many of the old Germanic tribes used horses for purposes of divination, believing the sacred beasts to be more in contact with the gods than were the priests. Charlemagne presented his four sons with the magical talking horse Bayard, whose back could stretch from a single saddle to accom-modate all four of its masters.

The horse was introduced to the Native American people by the Spanish explorers in the early 1500s. Although the strange, large animal had been foreseen in the visions of the Inca prophets of Viracocha in Peru, none of the people in South America were prepared for the actual meeting with the awesome creature. When the Inca people first encountered the

Spanish conquistadors, some believed the riders and their horses to be a single animal, a monster with a bearded human face and a body with four legs. Later, when the Inca were able to distinguish the Spanish invaders as humans, they recalled the words of their mystics who had warned of the destruction of the Inca culture at the hands of men with beards who would sit astride strange animals of great size and carry rods that would flash fire and death.

Coronado brought the first horses to the Plains Indians in 1541. Typical of the tribes along the routes of the early Spanish explorers, the Blackfeet had no words to describe the great steeds on which the armored strangers sat astride. They decided the mysterious four-legged beast looked more like an elk than anything else they had seen in their world, so they named the horse the Medicine Elk. Other tribes thought the horses looked more like big dogs, and they rubbed the animals' sweat on their own bodies in the hope of absorbing some of their strength.

Horses that strayed or escaped from the Spanish conquistadors formed the nucleus of great wild herds that revolutionized entire tribal cultures. Tribes that had settled near rivers and practiced a relatively stable and sedentary lifestyle were transformed into nomadic people in one or two generations. As horses enabled tribes to hunt in ever-expanding parameters, the likelihood of increased scrimmages and battles with other tribes greatly increased. And another tribe's horses were very often the prize of warfare.

The eastern tribes and the mighty Iroquois Confederacy did not have their visions of the strange animal fulfilled until the early 1600s when the first white settlers arrived from England. Horses reached the Nebraska tribes in the 1680s, and the upper Missouri by the 1750s.

The horse had long been a revered animal in Europe and Asia, and it soon became a sacred and prized possession of the Native American people. From the plains of the West to the forest trails of the East, the number of horses tethered outside a man's home became an indicator of his wealth. In only a few generations of human and equine interaction, the horse began to play a prominent role in tribal myths and legends, as well as in the determination of social status. At the same time that the horse became indispensable as a physical companion to the hunter and the warrior, the great four-legged animal also achieved a spiritual significance, just as the horse had done in Europe and Asia.

Sherry Hansen Steiger
Brad Steiger
Forest City, Iowa

*B*eth S. wrote to tell us about two special horses that she believed were really angels in disguise that protected, maybe even saved, the lives of her two little girls, Tonya, six, and Sonya, eight.

Beth was left with two young girls to raise when she and her husband were divorced five years ago. In spite of their attempts to work things out, spending years in and out of marital counseling sessions, reconciliation just wasn't happening.

"So the inevitable heartache occurred and we split up," Beth said sadly.

Agreeing that she and the girls would remain living in the area, Beth had tried in vain to locate a house in the same school district, but one that wasn't quite so remote as the one they owned in the country. Explaining that she was nervous about the isolation of the home, it was still the best option for the girls to remain in the same school, with as little disruption as possible.

"Although several of the marital counseling sessions included the girls, we wanted to make certain that they knew that none of the problems that mommy and daddy had been experiencing with each other had anything to do with them, nor was it their fault in any way," Beth said.

Beth went on to tell us that she and her husband hadn't expected that the girls would take it so hard, as they had included them in a number of counseling sessions. Naively, she understands now, they felt that the divorce shouldn't really have been a surprise to Tonya and Sonya. They had tried to prepare them and protect them at the same time, but when the final declaration was stated as fact, the girls refused to accept it and were in shock. In total denial, they refused to believe the divorce was going to happen. Tonya and Sonya were convinced their parents would work things out and be one happy family once again.

"They were so traumatized that we were scared for them—so much so that we took them to a child psychologist, suggested by our marital counselor," Beth shared.

Dr. J. was very helpful and assured Beth and her husband that this was a common reaction from many children going through a divorce situation.

She told the couple that the most important thing was to be consistent in assuring the girls that they were loved and always would be by both parents, no matter what. Beth said that the counselor's words had assuaged their fears and renewed hope that they could get through this.

In one of the several sessions, the idea of pet therapy was brought up as Dr. J. explained the theory behind it and of her successful applications of it with several difficult children patients.

"Elaborating on how pets could be among the best therapy for young and old alike, the doctor added that children often make smoother adjustments in times of crisis if they have a new 'dream' pet to love and care for," Beth said.

Even if it is on a subconscious level, many children think that if their parents broke a life-long commitment that they had made to each other, they, too, are expendable and could be next to be divorced. The love and care of a pet has been proven to lessen anxiety, promote healing, encourage the re-establishment of trust, and provide unconditional love, especially during times of crisis, the doctor suggested.

"We already had Prince, our black Labrador retriever, but I realized the children were too young when we first got him to have any sense of the process of caring for a pet in the way the doctor was suggesting, so I thought maybe a puppy that the girls picked out themselves would be just the ticket," Beth said. "After all, what is cuter than a puppy?

"Then," she continued, "the words the therapist had spoken—'dream pet'—really hit me. What was a dream pet?"

As the psychologist continued to talk about the importance of redirecting the children's focus, yet not skirting or ignoring their actual feelings, she answered Beth's unspoken question by asking if there was any special animal or pet that the girls talked about or admired.

This prompted Beth to remember that the school counselor had pointed out the seeming obsession the girls had with horses. Mentioning this to the child psychologist, she explained that she'd always simply dismissed this as a normal phase that all girls went through.

"I told Dr. J. that I thought the kids' fascination with horses would pass, and I didn't pay much attention to it, as I confessed how I, myself, went through such a stage as a young girl," Beth said. "I loved horses, and for at least four years had a horse blanket on my bed in the winter, horse posters on my wall, and horse trinkets everywhere. But, I grew out of it, especially when my mother and father told me they couldn't afford a horse; so, I figured it was a passing phase many girls go through, including mine."

For weeks following that session with Dr. J., Beth told us that if nothing else, the sparkle in Tonya's and Sonya's eyes at the mere discussion of horses was worth it, and it was fun sharing their common love of horses, even if it might indeed be a passing fancy. They went horseback riding and talked about how much fun it would be to have a horse, but Beth did her best to steer the girls' thoughts to a puppy when talking in terms of a new pet.

Tonya and Sonya were not interested in the slightest at even looking at puppies, so Beth tried to explain to them that the cost factor of having a horse made it impossible to buy one at this time.

"We had just come from church and as funny as this sounds now, it broke my heart then," Beth said. "From the backseat of the car, Tonya blurted out, 'God will get us a horse! The preacher said . . . anything you ask God for, if you believe . . . He'll give it to you.'"

Beth sighed, "What could I say to that, other than . . . let's pray about it."

They did pray about it, and God must have heard their prayers. On a Tuesday afternoon, Dr. J. called saying that she had clients whose changes in life circumstances forced them to downsize and that included two old horses they needed to get rid of. They emphasized that although the horses were twenty years old already, they couldn't bear to put them down, and they wondered if she knew of any family or children who might like to have them and who would take good care of them as they were such good and gentle horses.

Beth recalls, "It couldn't have been anything other than an answer to prayer. Even if the horses were up there in years, I knew in an instant that their age didn't matter. Something told me this would be a miracle for the girls. And as I said, we were out in the country with plenty of room for horses. Little did I know that these gift horses would prove to be lifesavers—not only of Tonya's and Sonya's hearts and souls, but of their very lives."

Beth told us that the girls named the two horses Night and Day, and they became like glue with the horses, hanging on them, talking to them, taking care of them. "Nearly to the point of overgrooming, if there is such a thing," Beth laughed. "They wanted to be with Night and Day every moment, day and night—they even wanted to sleep with them!"

One night, Prince started out-of-control barking. It woke Beth up, and she panicked as she raced into the girls' room and saw empty beds. "My heart raced a mile a beat to the point I thought I was having a heart attack, as I ran around screaming for the girls," Beth sighed. "I could still hear Prince barking, but I could not find him, either. Then, finally, I saw him, squeezed under an old overstuffed chair."

Running out to the horse shelter/minibarn that her ex-husband had helped to build along with the assistance of several friends, Beth saw Day and Night standing stalwart, but with a semiwild look in their eyes. They had positioned themselves so she could not get by, and that scared her even more.

Beth yelled out as loud as she could, calling for Tonya and Sonya, thinking something terrible had happened. Beth's thoughts went wild as she thought maybe the girls had sneaked out to sleep with the horses—who just might not have welcomed their company at night. And as they stood there with that strange look in their eyes, what if they harmed them?

Tonya and Sonya were on the floor behind Day and Night, cowering and shivering.

"Mommy, Mommy, Mommy," they both blurted out upon seeing her and hearing her calls.

The girls proceeded to rattle off jumbled details of the nightmare they'd just lived through. Neither one of them could sleep because they missed their horses so much, and they went out to sneak a little ride and then go back to bed.

"But the horses wouldn't go, Mommy," Sonya said excitedly. "They just stood there, not letting us get on, but nudging us to the corner. Then we saw a man come running up to the stall, and both Night and Day moved toward him and pushed him . . . bucking and pawing at him. We were way back in a corner of the stall, and the horses wouldn't let the man in. They kept on bucking and bucking, until he ran away—and then you came."

Tonya added that it was as though both Night and Day waited to start bucking until they knew the girls were at a safe-enough distance behind them and they wouldn't get hurt.

"Needless to say, I was filled with a mix of emotions," Beth expressed. "I was angry at the girls for even thinking of doing such a dangerous thing as going out there at night . . . *sneaking out* . . . at that.

"So we had a good talk about that, but mostly, I was relieved and elated that they were safe . . . that was the main thing, as I cried out with thanks to God," Beth emphasized. "The capper that I'm still amazed over, is what *could* have happened if the horses hadn't been their protectors."

Police cars soon showed up in response to Beth's calling 911 to report the incident. The officers informed her that on a neighboring property a woman had been beaten and robbed just an hour before.

"No doubt the man from whom the horses protected the girls was up to no good," Beth said, concluding her story. "A few hours later, with the help of dogs and a search party, the man was found, arrested, and evidence enough was obtained to incriminate him in the beating of the neighbor.

"Even the police said that our horses must be angels in disguise," Beth emphasized. "The girls and I *know* that is true!"

*D*uring the first week of August 2001, Sylvia Sebring of Tucson, Arizona, had a series of recurring dreams in which she saw a light gray mare standing in a corral at the Marana Stockyards. The horse had a pronounced limp, and, what was most unsettling, the mare was telepathically asking her for help.

Witnessing the plight of an injured horse was certainly not an unusual experience for Sylvia Sebring. She is a veterinary technician with the Tucson-based Castaway Treasures Animal Sanctuary, and she deals daily with suffering animals. But to dream repeatedly of a horse that was unknown to her and that clearly appeared to be asking for her personal help was a unique occurrence for her, and she would awaken drenched with sweat, experiencing anxiety and a tightness in her chest. What did the horse want her to do? And why had the dream creature sought her out?

She was certain that the local stockyards were the locale of the dream. As a veterinary technician, she had gone to the Marana Stockyards on many occasions to bid on distressed animals to take to the Sanctuary. But even though the scene of the dreams was very real, how could she translate the injured horse into a waking reality? What did the dream mean?

Sylvia Sebring consulted with friends and family members. Perhaps there was some symbolism in the dream that she was overlooking. But none of the people in her most trusted inner circle could shed any light on the troublesome nocturnal vision.

One day a friend of the Animal Sanctuary called to inform the staff that the U.S. Border Patrol had found some abandoned horses that had been left to die by drug smugglers in the desert near Arivaca. The concerned individual suggested that the Sanctuary might attempt to retrieve the forsaken animals.

On August 15, the *Tucson Citizen* carried a story about a horse that was not found until about a week after the other abandoned animals had been rescued. A U.S. Customs Service aircraft had sighted the mare lying nearly immobilized, its rear leg entangled in the stirrup rigging of its saddle. The horse had lain in the terrible heat of the desert with no water for at least a week. The newspaper story described the horse as a white Arabian mare, and stated that she had a twelve-inch cut on her left foreleg.

Ms. Sebring felt an eerie shock of recognition as she read about the mare found in the desert. The horse in her dream appeared to be light gray in color. A white horse that had been lying unattended in the desert might well appear to be gray. And what about the injured leg? That, too, seemed to fit her dream scenario. When Ms. Sebring counted back the days that the mare had lain abandoned, she realized that would have been the time when the dreams began. Could it be that the horse had been sending her desperate messages in her dreams that she needed to come and rescue it?

Prompted to do some investigation regarding the condition and present location of the rescued horses, Ms. Sebring learned that the animals were due to be auctioned September 6 at the Marana Stockyards. At this time, various individuals would bid for the horses, including buyers who attended such auctions for the sole purpose of obtaining inexpensive animals for resale to dog food packing plants.

When Sylvia Sebring first saw the Arabian mare in the corral at the stockyards, she knew immediately that the horse with the bulky bandage on its left foreleg was the same light-colored mare that she had seen in her dreams. Ms. Sebring knew that she had received the horse's cry for help, and she was there at the stockyards to answer that desperate entreaty.

Ms. Sebring told Paul Allen of the *Tucson Citizen* (September 12, 2001) that she had come there that day prepared to buy the horse and that she had already named the Arabian mare Dream Walker before she even set eyes on her.

Interestingly, there was an elderly couple in attendance at the auction that day who were also intent on rescuing the horses from the buyers who would sell them for dog food. They and Sylvia Sebring bid against each other unknowingly for the same humane motives when Dream Walker came into the auction ring, each believing the other to represent an ignoble demise for the mare. The couple finally dropped out of the bidding when it reached a total of $425, three times the amount that some of the other horses brought. At last, the outcry from an abandoned and injured horse that Sylvia Sebring heard in a troubled dream had been answered. She was now the pleased and proud owner of Dream Walker.

Ms. Sebring learned that Dream Walker was five or six years old, and she later determined that the mare would regain full use of her left foreleg. While other distressed and abused animals are usually adopted out of the Castaway

Treasures Animal Sanctuary after their injuries have been healed, Dream Walker will remain
as Sylvia Sebring's own personal horse.

We had lost touch with our friend Diane Chavanne for a few years, so we were quite surprised when she wrote from Florida in June 2003 to inform us that she had become quite an accomplished horseperson. "Horses are so intuitive it's really scary," she told us. "And they love and protect so willingly. It is difficult for me to imagine anyone hurting them."

Yet Diane bought her first horse under just such circumstances. "Duke was a fourteen-month-old stud colt that I found in a showbarn. He had been whipped, neglected, and isolated. I bought him on the spot just to remove him from those cruel conditions."

Diane spent months just showing Duke affection and love before she attempted to ride him. She felt that it was very important first to demonstrate to him that not all humans were cruel and brutal.

"Finally, I attempted to start him under saddle," Diane said, "and out of fear, he freaked while I was on him and he reared."

Duke threw his head back and caught Diane directly under her eye, knocking her unconscious. "With that sudden and unexpected blow from his powerful neck and hard equine head, I was knocked out cold in the saddle," Diane recalled. "I woke up facedown in the dirt."

Diane managed to unsaddle Duke and to make it slowly to the house. Friends were concerned that she might have suffered a concussion, so they kept Diane from resting in bed for several hours for fear that she might fall asleep. When at last it appeared the probable danger from a concussion had passed and Diane was left to deal with a major headache, she was allowed to fall asleep.

"When I awoke, I looked out the window and thought I was surely hallucinating from the aftershock of the fall," Diane said. "There on the front porch looking in at me was Duke!"

Diane opened the door to the porch and Duke pushed himself up against her in a big "hug." Then she walked him back to the barn.

"Duke had broken out of his stall, jumped a six-foot-high fence, and come from the back of the 2½-acre yard to the front of the house to look in the window to find me," Diane explained. "He knew that he had hurt me, and he had come to see if I was all right."

Diane also recalled the time that she had taken Duke to Alabama to spend some time during the winter months with a friend. "My friend slipped and fell on the ice, and Duke quickly slipped his neck under her arm and supported her while he walked her off the ice."

Diane also shared with us an amusing story about one of her show mares who loves to turn the lights off on Diane when she is out in the barn. "If I scold her, she'll turn them back on," Diane said.

This same show mare also has a habit of flapping her lips—what some old-timers called a "horse laugh"—when she is nervous and wishes to be comforted.

"One time the trainer put her in a trailer with about ten of his show stallions," Diane said. "We walked away for about half an hour, and when we returned, she had taught every one of the 'boys' how to flap their lips. We opened the trailer, and all eleven horses flapped their lips at us in unison."

Diane recalled that the horse trainer "about died." He said, "All we need is for one of them to flap their lips at the judges when they come by!"

On June 12, 2003, in the annual twenty-two-mile William Hill Man versus Horse Marathon held in Llanwrtyd Wells, Powys, mid-Wales, a horse won for the twentieth race in a row. After reading that opening sentence, a great sighing sound is probably heard across the world: "Duhhh. Four legs are always better and faster than two. Who would believe that a human could ever beat a horse in a foot race?"

Nonetheless, in spite of the disbelief on the part of the champions of horseflesh, William Hill offers odds of 25/1 that someday one of the human challengers can beat a horse to the finish line. And the never-claimed prize, which increases by 1,000 pounds every year, will reach a hefty 25,000 pounds for next year's race.

In 2003, thirty horses and their riders were pitted against nearly 400 runners and fifty relay teams.

Although there was much sweat and tears raised by the human racers determined to best their equine opponents, a horse named Druimgiga Shemal, ridden by Robyn Petrie-Richie, crossed the finish line to win the twenty-two-mile course in two hours and two minutes.

It must be noted that Druimgiga Shemal did have a rather close contender in thirty-eight-year-old Royal Marine Mark Croasdale, who had recently returned from serving in the Iraq conflict. Croasdale crossed the finish line in two hours and seventeen minutes. A confident runner who seems the likeliest challenger to accomplish what seems an impossible task, Croasdale has won the race against the human runners as a single human runner a total of six times.

*V*isitors still gather today at Claiborne Farm in Paris, Kentucky, to pay tribute to the great Triple Crown legend Secretariat, and to lay flowers on the grave. It is traditional to bury the head, heart, and hooves of a beloved horse, but when Secretariat died in 1989 he was given the honor of being buried whole in the cemetery of Claiborne Farm.

With his long legs, large-barreled chestnut-colored body, well-shaped head, and obvious intelligence, Secretariat has been proclaimed by many racing enthusiasts to be the exact image of a perfect racehorse. Secretariat was owned by Penny Tweedy, who had inherited Meadow Farm in Doswell, Virginia, from her father, Christopher Cheney. Born on March 30, 1970, Secretariat was the son of Bold Ruler out of the mare Something Royal, and the trainers took note of the fact that Secretariat was an independent-minded entity from the very beginning. Ms. Tweedy also recognized that she had a confident and curious colt on her hands, one that was already leaving his mother's side to explore pastures on his own.

Secretariat's first race gave little indication of the magnificent master of the racetrack that he was to become. He got off to a bad start right out of the gate at Aqueduct on July 4, 1972, and finished fourth. That ill-fated start at the gate and a disqualification at the Champagne Stakes at Belmont would be his only losses in a two-year career that would see Secretariat win eight straight races. In 1972, Secretariat received the Horse of the Year Award. The media, racing fans, horse owners, even his fellow competitors considered him one of the most remarkable horses to set foot on the turf.

Secretariat's owner and trainers began to prepare him for the Triple Crown, the highest goal in professional horse racing. First would come the Kentucky Derby, then the Preakness, and third, the Belmont Stakes. Secretariat would have only one opportunity to claim the title of the Triple Crown, for he had been syndicated into shares by Claiborne Farm, and his future breeding rights sold for $6,080,000—an enormous sum for the time. Included in the agreement was a clause that allowed Secretariat to race only through his three-year-old season, so for the gallant horse and his owner, Penny Tweedy, 1973 was a year of destiny that would either bring blazing glory or a disappointing run into retirement.

At the 1973 Kentucky Derby, Secretariat and Angle Light were the favorites, with Sham gaining support as the second choice. Secretariat broke from the gate without difficulty, but he soon found himself running in last place. Sham became the leader and moved several lengths away from the pack. Some spectators began to shout encouragement for Secretariat while others in the stands grumbled about a major racing upset that would cost them plenty.

Secretariat stayed in last place for what seemed an agonizing eternity for those who had come to cheer him to victory. Then, horse by horse, Secretariat moved ahead until he was racing neck and neck with Sham. Jockey Ron Turcotte confidently signaled the chestnut colt to make his play, and Secretariat won the Kentucky Derby by 2½ lengths, setting a new track record.

In many ways, the Preakness was a replay of the Kentucky Derby. Although Secretariat was the favorite after his win at the Derby, to the great consternation of thousands of racing fans, he once again seemed contented to run in last place. While the spectators watched in amazement and cheered themselves hoarse, Secretariat steadily passed horse after horse, winning the second race of the Triple Crown by 2½ lengths. In addition, Secretariat finished the Preakness with a time of 1:55, a full second off the Kentucky Derby track record. However, the clockers from *The Daily Racing Form* claimed that they had recorded Secretariat's time crossing the wire as 1:53 2/5, thereby shattering the Derby record and raising a controversy over the actual official time, which still flares in racing circles today. Sham once again came across the wire in second place.

At the Belmont Stakes, the final race in the Triple Crown, the vast crowd that gathered speculated whether or not Secretariat and jockey Turcotte would employ the same risky strategy of running in last place before accelerating into mind-boggling record speed. Only five horses had qualified to run in the Belmont Stakes, and Sham, the second-place winner at the Kentucky Derby, was certain to give Secretariat another good run for the money.

When the horses broke from the starting gate, Secretariat chose not to waste a moment of time and ran straight to the front. Sham stayed ahead of the pack with him through the first turn, and it appeared that the crowd was going to witness a two-horse race right up to the finish line. However, by the time Secretariat reached the backstretch, he had already achieved a ten-length lead over Sham. As the racing enthusiasts shouted their astonishment, Secretariat came down the homestretch with what appeared to be a lead of twenty-two lengths. When he crossed the finish line, it was declared that he had won the Belmont Stakes, the final race in the Triple Crown, by an incredible thirty-one lengths and set a new world record of 2:24.

As he neared his three-year retirement cutoff, Secretariat had earned his owner an estimated $1,316,808—a record sum at that time.

Before he retired to the pastures and stables of Claiborne Farm in Paris, Kentucky, to live out the remainder of his life as a stud, the Marlboro company sponsored a last race between Secretariat and his stablemate, River Ridge. This two-horse contest would be no easy dust-off for Secretariat. River Ridge had won the Kentucky Derby and the Belmont Stakes the previous year, and racing insiders speculated that the mighty Secretariat could enter retirement with a loss marring his remarkable track record. Destiny, however, had ordained that Secretariat would leave the world of racing as a great champion. He not only won the race against River Ridge by 3½ lengths, he set a new world's record.

When Secretariat arrived at Claiborne Farm to begin his retirement, more than 6,000 fans and admirers of fine horses came by to say their good-byes. The Triple Crown legend died in 1989 of laminitis, an incurable foot disease.

*C*harlie W., who lived in a small town in southern Minnesota, wrote to tell us of the time that his easily spooked Buckskin mare Nacho truly proved her merit and courage.

"Ever since Nacho was a filly just a few months old, she would jump at nearly everything," Charlie told us. "Her mother was Lady Claudette, who was named after my father's grandmother, a woman, according to Dad, of great elegance. Lady Claudette was a good-natured Buckskin of typical coloration for that breed, kind of a dun-color, and she had a rich black mane. Nacho was sired by a Palomino named Gold Charger, so when she was just a foal she seemed almost yellow in color, and I named her Nacho. Later, it seemed that I had named her well because she jumped at every snap and crackle in the horse barn."

Charlie explained that his family were not breeders or trainers, but simply farm folk who delighted in keeping horses to supplement the standard animal citizenry of cattle, chicken, and pigs. They were also a family who enjoyed riding horses and occasionally going on weekend trail rides with groups of other horse lovers.

"In addition to Nacho and Lady Claudette, we also had a gelding, a reliable old quarter horse named Sam, who was about twenty years old at the time Nacho was born," Charlie said.

Charlie recalled that he graduated from high school in May of 1973 when Nacho was around two years old. "I spent a lot of time with her that summer," he explained, "because I would be leaving for college in September, and I wanted to ride her when I came home on weekends and holidays. After a lot of patience on my part, Nacho had been broken to saddle, and my father, sister Stacy, and I had all ridden her around the farm. We all agreed that she responded well to a light touch on the reins and that she was a nice riding horse."

There was still the problem of her skittishness, however. "Sometimes Nacho would begin to bolt if a squawking rooster ran across her path," Charlie said. "If I wasn't paying attention to business, there were times that Nacho nearly threw me when Bosco, our terrier, barked at a rabbit."

When Charlie's older sister Tracy visited that July with her three-year-old daughter Alana in tow, there occurred an incident involving Nacho that could have had a very tragic ending.

"Tracy's husband Randy is a motorcycle enthusiast," Charlie said. "He was away attending some annual motorcycle rally, and he planned to join Tracy and Alana on the farm in a couple of days after the event was over. We had no idea that he had invited three of his buddies to camp out overnight before they continued on to their own homes."

Charlie recalled that on that fateful day he was on the tractor cultivating corn in the field next to the horse and cattle pasture. "I had seen Tracy and Stacy riding horses around the pasture and then taking them out on the gravel road for a few miles. Stacy was riding Nacho and Tracy was riding Lady Claudette, with little Alana wedged in between her mother and the saddle horn. I thought this was great. The girls were riding together just like they did when they were kids. Over the noisy hum of the tractor's engine, I could almost hear Alana giggling and shouting for her mother to go faster."

Charlie had stopped for a coffee break and had shut off his tractor for a few moments' quiet when he looked to see where his sisters and little niece were riding. "I spotted them down the lane leading to the road," he said. "They had switched rides, and now Tracy and Alana were on Nacho. I didn't think this was such a good idea. I hoped that Stacy had explained how easily Nacho could be spooked. If Tracy were riding solo, that would be fine. She could handle a jumpy horse by herself. But I got really nervous when she was in the saddle with one arm around little Alana."

Charlie's apprehensions were intensified when he heard a roaring sound that could come from only one thing on Earth: a motorcycle. And as he scanned the road to better pinpoint the thunder of engines, Charlie was surprised to see four big Harley-Davidsons churning up massive clouds of dust on the gravel road. Then he panicked when he saw the four "hogs" about to enter the lane, less than thirty yards from the two horses and their riders.

"I have never been so frightened or filled with terror as that terrible moment when I thought how Nacho would respond to four thunderous motor-cycles charging down the lane," Charlie said. "She would be likely to rear and throw Tracy and Alana."

And then Charlie saw something that nearly made his heart stop. "Tracy had dismounted to wave at Randy and to prepare to give him a welcoming hug—and she had left little Alana sitting alone on the saddle on Nacho's back."

Charlie felt helpless. "I shouted at Tracy to grab Alana off Nacho, but I knew that there was no way she could hear me over the roar of the approaching motorcycles. I got off the tractor and just started running toward Nacho and Alana. I knew that I could never get there in time to get her off Nacho before the horse spooked and threw her, but I just didn't know what else to do."

Charlie could see that his father, who was doing some repair work on his tractor in the machine shed, had also begun to run toward what he, too, had likely assumed would be a scene of potential tragedy.

In horror and astonishment, Charlie saw the four motorcyclists approach within a hair's breadth of Nacho and Alana. Oblivious to the danger of spooking a horse and its rider, the cheering, laughing cyclists were showing off what they perceived to be their own prowess on wheels.

"And this was the miracle, the wonderful thing," Charlie said. "Nacho stood as still as a statue. She didn't flinch a muscle. Somehow, in some marvelous way, she was aware of the precious bundle of humanity on her back. By some transmission of knowledge that mere human intelligence could never perceive, Nacho knew that there was a helpless little girl seated in the saddle. As if an angel had whispered in her ear and blessed her with tranquility, Nacho had become a rock of safety for Alana."

As might be expected of any horse faced with the near-approach of roaring motorcycles, Lady Claudette shied away from the men and their vehicles and began to sidestep nervously. Stacy had her reins in hand and began working to calm and steady her.

Charlie's eyes teared as he continued to run toward Nacho and her little rider. "This was the horse that was spooked by the clanging of a milk pail, by the sudden movement of chickens scratching in the dirt, by the barking of a dog," he said. "Now, amidst the thunderous roar of four Harley-Davidsons, she stood steel nerved and unflinching."

Charlie's father reached the scene before he did, and he snatched Alana from the saddle. For the first time, Tracy seemed to become aware of the danger that could have caused her daughter a terrible fall—or worse.

"Dad handed Alana to Tracy," Charlie said, "and then, after Randy and his buddies had shut off their bikes, in no uncertain terms he really laid into the men about the careless, thoughtless behavior of approaching two farm horses used to peace and quiet with the noisy roar of motorcycles. Dad pointed out that Alana could have been badly hurt, even killed, and Tracy and Stacy could easily have been thrown or injured. Within a few minutes, Dad had those men unable to look either him or Alana in the eye. In another minute or so, Randy and his crew were sheepishly apologizing to anyone who would listen. Tracy was crying and hugging Alana as if she would never again let her go. Stacy was still trying to settle Lady Claudette and at the same time she was berating herself for having been so forgetful and careless."

Charlie put his arms around Nacho and hugged her neck. "I kept praising Nacho over and over again," he said. "I told her I was so proud of her and that I loved her."

It was then that Charlie felt Nacho trembling. He looked into her eyes and saw that she was wild with fear. "She knew that she had a duty to the little girl on her back, and she performed the unspoken obligation to its owner that a devoted horse will always strive its very best to fulfill. But in spite of her courage and her love, she was frozen, paralyzed with terror."

Charlie said that he lifted himself into the saddle and rode Nacho for nearly an hour, "to let off steam and nervous energy." The spooky, flighty horse that was Nacho had been reborn as a courageous and stalwart animal.

Although Charlie did not become a farmer, when he graduated from college and accepted a teaching position, he moved Nacho to a stable in the city where he taught high school. The two friends continued to bond and develop a deep, loving relationship. Each of Charlie's three children learned to ride on Nacho, who died in 2000, at twenty-nine years of age.

*L*akota elders tell of the deep friendship that developed between Jumping Badger and a beautiful white horse that could dance. Jumping Badger, a member of the Lakota tribe, was born about 1834 in what is present-day South Dakota. After a fierce battle with the white pony soldiers in 1857, a medicine vision told Jumping Badger to change his name, and it is as Sitting Bull that the great Hunkpapa Teton Lakota (Sioux) chief and medicine man is known in the white people's history books.

In the mid-1870s, Sitting Bull had a powerful vision that the combined force of many tribes would be able to defeat the cavalry units that were being deployed against them by the U.S. government to defend the settlers and the gold hunters. After the victory of the amassed tribal warriors over General George Armstrong Custer's 7th cavalry battalion at the Little Big Horn on June 25, 1876, Sitting Bull's reputation as a seer became as revered among the other Plains tribes as it was among the Lakota.

To escape revenge by U.S. troopers after the crushing defeat of the Seventh Cavalry at the Little Big Horn, Sitting Bull and his people crossed the border into Canada. There, the medicine chief told Canadian journalists that he had never declared war on the United States, but the soldiers, settlers, and prospectors had invaded his land and forced him to fight to protect his people's hunting grounds.

In 1881, Sitting Bull surrendered to the U.S. Army and was confined at Fort Randall until 1883. Upon his release, Buffalo Bill invited him to join his famous touring Wild West Show and Circus. It was while performing across the eastern United States, Great Britain, and Europe that Sitting Bull met the beautiful white horse with which he seemed to unite in spirit.

Buffalo Bill Cody had seen to it that the magnificent steed had been well trained in all the maneuvers required of a dramatic performance in a Wild West show. When gunfire broke out during one of the acts performed in the arena in front of the grandstand, the horse would arch its neck and prance. It would shake its long mane, bend to paw the ground, then rear up and leap in the air. Since it had been trained to perform these motions rapidly while prancing, snorting, cantering, and moving in a circle, many people in the bleachers shouted their excitement and amusement at watching what appeared to be a dancing horse. Since Sitting Bull seemed to admire the grace and skill of the animal, Buffalo Bill assigned the horse to the medicine man during the time of his association with the Wild West Show.

One of the acts in the show that was always a crowd-pleaser from New York to London featured a stagecoach being chased by whooping warriors and being rescued by the U.S. cavalry. Rifles, revolvers, and shotguns in the hands of stagecoach drivers, passengers, and pony soldiers fired dozens of blank cartridges and expert tribal marksmen launched arrows that purposely missed their targets. Sitting Bull's role in the performance was essentially to be himself. He rode into the arena bedecked in his most colorful regalia, riding upon the white horse to receive the thunderous applause of the audience. By his appearance in Buffalo Bill's Wild West Show, Sitting Bull's image had been transformed from a bloodthirsty savage to that of a wise medicine man and chief who became a very popular figure throughout the United States and Europe.

Around 1888, Sitting Bull made the decision to leave Buffalo Bill's show and return to his people. As a gesture of their friendship, Buffalo Bill gave Sitting

Bull the majestic white horse that he had ridden in countless performances in the Wild West Show.

Sitting Bull became fascinated by the teachings of Wovoka, a Piute prophet, who had introduced the Ghost Dance religion to the native people. Wovoka promised a new age when the buffalo would return and the old traditions would be restored. Many of the Sioux began to put on the ghost shirts and sought to dance back the old days from the land of the spirits. Sitting Bull became an impassioned leader of the new religion, and he implored his people not to forget their culture and their religion. He said that they must never forsake their own language and their worship of the Great Spirit.

On a cold winter's day in December 1890, soldiers arrived on the reservation at Wounded Knee with orders to arrest Sitting Bull for preaching resistance to the federal government. Sitting Bull resisted and many of his followers began to fight the soldiers.

As shots rang out, Sitting Bull's white horse began to respond to the sounds of a gun battle that were so familiar to it from its years in the Wild West Show. As bullets whizzed all around it, the white horse began to dance. With a practiced grace, the horse arched its neck, pranced, reared up, and cantered around and around in a circle. When the sounds of gunfire ceased, the beautiful white horse continued to dance until it was exhausted.

Then the horse faced the scene of the battle where Sitting Bull and fifteen of his people lay dead. Breathing heavily and lathered with sweat in spite of the cold, the white horse extended its left foreleg and bowed toward his master. It is a legend among the Lakota that the beautiful white horse danced in Sitting Bull's honor on the day that the great leader was killed.

For many Native American tribes, to see a vision of a great, white horse is to have seen the symbol of Death coming to take one to the land of the Grandparents.

The Muslims have their *Al Borak*, a milk-white steed whose single stride can propel him as far as the farthest range of human vision. Slavic legends tell of Prince Slugobyl, who enlists the aid of the Invisible Knight and his horse Magu (magus, wizard), a magical white horse with a golden mane.

Kwan-yin in China and Kuannan in Japan materialize as white horses. The Hindu god Vishnu's final manifestation will occur when he reappears on a white horse with a drawn sword to restore the order of righteousness. The Book of Revelation says that Christ shall return riding upon a white horse and leading armies of righteousness seated upon white horses.

It is interesting to take note of world culture and perceive that the association of a white horse with an ethereal and holy task seems to have assumed the status of a universal image.

*W*hen horses are bored, frustrated, or under stress, they commonly engage in a behavior called weaving, in which they sway their heads from side to side. Daniel Mills, a Principal Lecturer at the Animal Behavior, Cognition and Welfare Group at the University of Lincoln, near Grantham, Lincolnshire, U.K., terms weaving a sign of social isolation that occurs when horses are kept for long periods of time alone in their stables.

Many horse owners seek to prevent their animals from weaving by erecting metal bars within the stables to restrict movement. But Dr. Jonathan Cooper, a senior lecturer at the group at Lincolnshire School of Agriculture, warns that horses in social isolation will only be made more frustrated and irritable by the presence of bars in their stables. The enforced limitation of their movement will only cause them to want to weave more and the horses will exhibit symptoms of even greater stress.

The scientists recognize that most horse owners are well intentioned, but they do their horses a great disservice if they isolate them. "Although most horse owners are well-meaning, they don't always do the best thing for the horse," Mills told Jenny Jarvie of the London *Telegraph* (September 9, 2001). Horses should never be treated as if they are machines, Mills advised, and they should never be kept in social isolation.

Then, in response to concern among horse owners about the well-being of their animals, the research group at the University of Lincoln came up with what may be at least a temporary solution to the problem of equine weaving. They discovered that horses may be made to feel happier and more relaxed if mirrors are fitted inside their stables. After fitting acrylic mirrors to the stable walls, the researchers found that frustrated horses that were experiencing the stress of social isolation by weaving, stopped such behavior or considerably reduced it within twenty-four hours.

Mills commented that some of the horses in their test sample had been exhibiting weaving behavior for six years. Once the mirrors were placed in their stables, these same bored and distressed horses ceased their weaving almost instantly.

It remains unclear to the researchers at the Cognition and Welfare Group exactly why the placement of mirrors in the horses' stables reduces weaving. Perhaps, they suggest, the horse's reflection in the mirror mimics visual contact with other horses and minimizes the feeling of social isolation within the stable. Another possibility is that the sight of its reflection may act as a distraction and thereby reduce the horse's perception that it is being isolated and confined.

Continued study revealed that the horses with the mirrors in their stables spent about a quarter of their time facing their reflection. Researchers learned that time spent in front of the mirrors did little to affect the proportion of time the horse invested in gazing out the stable door or sleeping. Interestingly, when the mirrors were removed, the horses did not immediately resume the weaving behavior that was indicative of their feelings of frustration and isolation.

The scientists admonished any horse owners who wished to place a mirror in their horse's stable to alleviate weaving behavior problems to be certain to use only a shatterproof reflective surface. Glass mirrors should never be used.

*W*hen Los Angeles architect William Hankins, thirty-nine, first arrived at the Santa Rosa Ranch in Douglas, Arizona, he was a complete greenhorn who had no experience with horses. During the first few trail rides, the cowboys gave Hankins an older quarter horse named Smoke, a gentle gelding that was patient with greenhorns and whose days of fierce galloping off toward the horizon were over. Hankins sensed that the horse was being extra kind to him, even looking out for him in an equine kind of way, so he repaid the favor by lavishing attention on Smoke and bringing him several apples a day as a special treat.

Toward the end of Hankins's stay at the ranch, he felt confident enough to leave the company of the ranch's cowhand escorts and his fellow big city greenhorns on the trail rides. He informed the cowboys at the horse corrals that he wanted to ride farther away from the main area by himself in order to explore the surrounding desert country. A couple of the cowboys acknowledged that Hankins had greatly improved his horsemanship, and he was given Thunder, a strong young horse, to ride.

Within a few hours, horse and rider were far from familiar terrain in a deep canyon. Hankins was completely absorbed in the beauty of the environment that was so very different from the concrete canyons of Los Angeles. For a minute or two, he was able to daydream that he was a working cowboy, looking for strays from the herd. In his imagination, he said later, he was lost in a fantasy of a time long past and the romance of a life that was completely foreign to a modern urban dweller.

Then he was suddenly snapped forward into an unfamiliar present as he became aware that his horse was experiencing difficulty negotiating the loose shale of the canyon—and he was completely uncertain how to handle the animal when it started slipping. Thunder bolted, desperately shuffling his back legs on the crumbling rock to remain upright. Then the big horse twisted his body as he found firm footing, and Hankins was thrown from the saddle.

He landed hard on the rocks of the canyon, and Thunder, freed of the rider and the unwelcome weight, galloped away and left him. Hankins felt dazed and confused. Wasn't a faithful steed always supposed to remain at the side of a downed rider?

Then it dawned on him that he and Thunder had not really had a great deal of time to bond in the approximately three hours they had known one another. The horse felt absolutely no allegiance to the greenhorn who sat in the saddle so awkwardly and with so little confidence. Now if it had been old Smoke, Hankins mused, he wouldn't have left him alone to face the doubtful mercies of the desert.

Soon after he realized that there was no way Thunder was coming back for him, Hankins made another very painful discovery. He had hurt his ankle very badly. He couldn't even stand, much less walk on it. He was in a very bad situation, because the area was full of rattlesnakes and mountain lions. What was even worse, he wasn't likely to be missed for many hours—perhaps even a day or more.

But help came to Hankins from an unexpected source. Back at the ranch, Smoke began acting restless in the corral. One of the cowhands asked his buddy what was wrong with the old fellow. "Danged if I know," the other replied. "He's generally the quietest horse of the bunch."

In the next few moments, much to the amazement of the ranch hands, Smoke had broken down a section of the corral and had taken off across the high chapparal in a dead run.

One of the men shouted to the other that they had to saddle up fast and bring old Smoke back to the corral before the other horses had a notion that they could take off like he did without so much as a by-your-leave or a so-long-it's-been-good-to-know-you.

To their complete amazement, there was no way that they could catch up to Smoke. It was as if the old-timer had been rejuvenated and transformed himself from a worn-out, long-in-the-tooth quarter horse into a young and sassy thoroughbred Kentucky Derby qualifier. And Smoke seemed to know exactly where he was going, so the men could only follow in angry pursuit.

"When Smoke found me, there were two hot and boiling-mad cowboys chasing him," Hankins said. "Their anger soon changed to astonishment when they saw that Smoke had led them directly to a ranch guest who was in terrible trouble. It became clear to all of us that he had broken out of his corral to come to rescue me.

"It was a strange kind of miracle," Hankins added. "Smoke was the first horse that I had learned to ride when I arrived at the Santa Rosa Ranch. I would always make a fuss over him, and we became good friends. Soon after I fell, it seems that he broke out of his corral and set off to cover the seven or eight miles to where I was."

That night, after a doctor had seen to his ankle, William Hankins presented Smoke with a special reward: a large bag of apples.

*I*n 1928, the feats of an apparently ordinary horse that seemed to be able to read, work complicated problems in mathematics, and communicate with human beings served as a major topic of conversation for millions of Americans. Lady, a three-year-old mare owned by Mrs. Claudia D. Fonda of Richmond, Virginia, was able to pick out the correct numbers in answer to arithmetic problems and to select alphabet blocks to spell out words in response to conversational questions. By nudging forward the proper blocks, Lady was able to carry on a dialogue with anyone who desired to question her.

For over a month, Lady was thoroughly studied for paranormal abilities by Dr. J. B. Rhine of Duke University and Dr. William McDougall, a leading psychologist. The two scientists conducted an amazing series of tests with the seemingly gifted black-

and-white horse. Even with Mrs. Fonda removed from the scene and with a screen placed between the horse and the researchers, Lady was able to answer all questions asked of her.

Later Mrs. Fonda and certain researchers developed a "typewriter" on which the letters of the alphabet and the numbers one to nine and zero were arranged in front of the mare, facing the questioners, not Lady. The talented horse was able to operate this communications device by lowering her muzzle onto levers that would flip up the letters or numbers to provide the answers to the queries directed at her. Such rapid and unerring facility led Dr. Rhine to conclude that animals were able to read the thoughts of humans via some extrasensory capacity.

In a *New York Times* article of May 28, 1928, the writer noted that it seemed a bit unkind to declare Lady a telepathic horse. "This makes it seem," he pointed out, "that Lady performs her miracles merely by mind reading, whereas the investigations might prove that she understands English and arithmetic on her own account."

It does appear, however, as though Lady's most remarkable attributes lay in her seeming powers of prophecy and clairvoyance. Associated Press reporter Paul Duke was astonished when Lady revealed his name, birthplace, and the correct amount of his salary.

It is a matter of documented record that Lady correctly predicted the names of the winners in various heavyweight boxing championship bouts, the entry of the United States and the Soviet Union into World War II, and President Franklin D. Roosevelt's third term in office. Her only notable miss was when she foresaw Thomas Dewey defeating Harry S. Truman in 1948. Asked to explain her inaccurate prognostication, Lady answered: "Funny, he too sure."

Some investigators considered Lady's most remarkable feat to be her role in helping to determine the fate of missing children. When four-year-old Danny Mason was lost in Quincy, Massachusetts, on a harshly cold day in January of 1951, the police were unable to turn up the slightest clue of his whereabouts. Family friends visited Lady the Wonder Horse and asked the sensitive mare for her assistance. Lady spelled out *Pittsfield Water Wheel,* which District Attorney Edmund R. Dewing and his staff of detectives sorted out to mean *Pit Field Wilde Water.* When the authorities dragged the Field-Wilde quarry, they found little Danny's body.

In another tragic instance, two children disappeared near Naperville, Illinois, in the winter of 1952–53. When one of the mothers of the missing children came to ask Lady Wonder for help, the horse went to her "typewriter" and stated that the woman would find her son's body in the river near their home. Authorities had already dragged the river, and the consensus among the searchers deemed one of two quarries to be the location of the children's bodies. Great expense was incurred in order to drain both quarries, but the children's bodies were discovered several months later in the nearby river where Lady the Wonder Horse had "seen" them.

In February 1946, when Lady was twenty-one years old, Dr. Thomas L. Garrett, a psychologist and editor-in-chief of *Your Mind,* a monthly psychology digest, visited the mare in the company of Lesley Kuhn, managing editor of the magazine. The two psychologists claimed that they had exposed many mind-reading and fortune-telling acts and that they were eager to encounter the famous wonder horse. After several visits, Dr. Garrett told the Norfolk, Virginia, *Virginia Pilot* (February 26, 1946) that he and his colleague were convinced that there was no trickery involved in Lady's acclaimed abilities. "I find Lady Wonder perfectly amazing," he said. "There is unquestionably genuine phenomena on the part of the horse."

In mid-March of 1957, Lady Wonder suffered a heart attack, and on March 19 she died. A group of about thirty mourners joined Mrs. Fonda at the funeral in Michael's Road Pet Cemetery in Henrico County.

The most controversial animal experiments of the early twentieth century began with a retired mathematics teacher of Elberfeld, Germany, named Wilhelm Von Osten, who had claimed to teach his Russian stallion, Clever Hans, to perform mathematical computations, tell time, and compose intelligent sentences. Thousands of spectators and scientists came to Clever Hans's stall to observe countless demonstrations of the horse's alleged abilities. While many official commissions and committees left Elberfeld completely convinced by what they had seen, just as many left expressing their disbelief.

Von Osten died in 1909 and bequeathed Hans to his friend Karl Krall, a wealthy jeweler, who had come to accept the mathematician's theories about the high intelligence of animals and the training of horses to think and to compute. Krall decided to provide classmates to keep Clever Hans company. He bought two Arabian stallions named Muhamed and Zarif, a blind pony named Berto, and a Shetland pony christened Hanschen. Krall discovered that Von Osten's training methods, combined with a few innovations of his own, soon produced wonder horses that were able to count, add, subtract, multiply, use decimals, read, spell, and respond to questions in a simplified language that he had developed for them to use. Generally, the talking horses gave their answers by stamping with their hooves in various codes developed by Krall.

Krall found it most interesting that Muhamed, perhaps the more intelligent of the Arabians, soon began to communicate spontaneously. When Krall entered the stable, Muhamed would sometimes tattle that the groom had beaten Hanschen or that one of the other animals had misbehaved. Sometimes he would even scold his partner, Zarif, for being lazy.

Once, when the horses were asked to give the cube root of 5,832, one of them stamped out the correct answer—18—while a committee of university scholars were still figuring out the solution on paper.

Controversy over the famous "Talking Horses of Elberfeld" spilled over from the universities and gave all of turn-of-the-century Europe a topic for passionate argument regarding the limits of animal intelligence and training. Such passionate disagreements over the true abilities of the Elberfeld stallions developed in France, Germany, and England that a special commission was appointed to investigate the actual nature of their intellectual capacities. Could these specially trained horses actually compute mathematical problems and spell out the answers to complicated philosophical questions? Professor Edward Claparede, a noted Swiss psychologist from the University of Geneva, Switzerland, declared the revelation of the "talking horses" to be the most sensational event that had ever appeared in the field of animal psychology—perhaps in the whole realm of psychology.

Professor Claparede, one of the leading European authorities on animal psychology, concluded that the Elberfeld stallions were not fakes and that they read and spelled and extracted cube roots by rational processes rather than by means of trick signs from their trainer. Dr. Claparede expressed his opinion that the horses were able to perform many of the tasks which might be required of an intelligent schoolboy of fourteen. The psychologist emphasized that he could find nothing whatever to the idea that their owner, Karl Krall, signaled the horses either consciously or unconsciously.

But other scientists and scholars objected to the very nature of the phenomenon and found it unlikely that the brains of mere horses could breech the distance between the whole pastoral existence of a horse and the abstract and impenetrable life of numbers. How could these horses interest themselves in signs and symbols that should represent nothing to their existence? Surely, they were completely ignorant of the consequences of the mathematical problems that they solved and somehow merely received the solutions as indifferently as a calculator. Or, perhaps they divined the answers from some great cosmic mystery?

Maurice Maeterlinck, the famous Belgian poet, playwright, and essayist, was among the scholars who traveled to Elberfeld to investigate Krall's famous thinking horses. Maeterlinck stated that he had investigated the phenomenal animals with the same scrupulous attention that he would have given to a criminal trial.

Maeterlinck wrote that when he saw the horses, he spoke the first word that came to his mind, *Weidenhof*, the name of his hotel. Muhamed immediately "wrote" *Weidenhov*. At this point Krall entered the stable and admonished Muhamed for making an error in spelling. The horse at once tapped out the *f*.

Maeterlinck was greatly impressed by Krall's obvious love for his pupils and the atmosphere of affection that he had created for the horses. "In a manner of speaking," the Belgian poet wrote in *The Unknown Guest*, "he has humanized them. There are no longer those sudden movements of panic which reveal the ancestral dread of man."

Maeterlinck observed that Krall spoke to the animals in a tender manner, as a loving father might speak to his children. "We have the strange feeling that they listen to all he says and understand it. If they appear not to grasp an explanation or demonstration, he will begin it all over again, analyze it, paraphrase it ten times in succession, with the patience of a mother."

A Dr. Hamel once gave Muhamed the number 7,890,481 and challenged the stallion to produce its fourth root. Within an astonishing six seconds, Muhamed had tapped out the answer, 53. Dr. Hamel checked with a table and was stunned to find that Muhamed was correct. It required eighteen multiplications, ten subtractions, and three divisions to extract the fourth root of a seven-figure number. Muhamed, a "dumb" animal, had managed those thirty-one calculations in six seconds.

Sadly, the incredible Elberfeld horses vanished as draft animals in the horror and gore of World War I. Hanschen, it is said, was eaten during the terrible famine.

In July 1955, Dr. William MacKenzie of Genoa University, president of the Italian Society of Parapsychology, was asked if he remembered the Elberfeld horses from the early days of the century. "Could

I forget!" he answered immediately. The only explanation that Dr. MacKenzie could offer was that the famous talking horses were "mediums," possessed by a reasoning mind superior to their own.

Eighty years after their remarkable feats, researchers still argue the intelligence of the Elberfeld horses. Geoffrey Cowley, writing in the May 23, 1988, issue of *Newsweek*, suggested that there was more to the story of Clever Hans and the training methods of Wilhelm Von Osten. A young psychologist named Oskar Pfungst supposedly made the discovery that although Hans succeeded on nine out of ten problems if the interrogator knew the answers, his score plummeted to just one out of ten if the questioner was ignorant of the correct sum.

"Further studies showed that [Hans] had learned to read minds by monitoring subtle changes in [the interrogators'] posture, breathing, and facial expressions," Cowley writes. "So keen was his sense of these cues that informed questioners couldn't conceal them if they tried. Hans could always tell when it was time to stop tapping or moving his head."

Noting that eighty-years-later disclaimer, Cowley nevertheless admits that "[scientists] are acknowledging that while Clever Hans might not have learned math, the knowledge he displayed was awesome just the same."

*M*onty Roberts, called by some the original "horse whisperer," has worked out a technique whereby a wild stallion can be convinced to accept bridle, saddle, and rider in just thirty minutes—without breaking the horse's spirit. Roberts's methods, while quite at odds with more conventional methods of "breaking" a horse, have been developed from years of observing the behavior of wild mustangs on the southwestern desert country and seeing how a dominant mare would deal with a troublesome foal until its temperament improved. Roberts proves his beliefs time and time again by demonstrating how he can communicate with a horse in its own language and gain its trust and respect.

Rather than saddling an untrained horse and riding it until it is "broken" or tying a horse to a post and binding its legs to force it to submit to human will, Roberts can get a previously unridden horse to accept saddle and bridle in less than an hour. He claims that there is nothing mystical about his methods. It is just plain horse sense, horse logic, and the ability to listen to what the horse is telling its owner.

Lynn Henry, who has a horse farm at Bramhope, West Yorkshire, U.K., isn't a horse whisperer, but rather, as she phrases it, a "horse listener." Some years ago, Ms. Henry had a great deal of trouble with a horse named Willow that simply wouldn't allow itself to be tacked up or tied up without problems. Rather than give up on the whole horse-riding business, Ms. Henry decided to learn all that she could about horse psychology. It was while learning to handle Willow and another very aggressive horse that Lynn Henry discovered Parelli Natural Horsemanship (PNH), an American system of training horses by utilizing equine language and psychology, rather than the old methods of using force to make a horse submit to its owner's wishes. Simply put, PNH asks that riders and trainers learn to think like a horse before they think like humans. The PNH techniques encourage those who would interact with horses to attempt to go back and observe the horse in the wild and do one's best to perceive how it lives and how it exercises its survival instinct as it interacts with other animals.

To demonstrate the success of the Parelli method, Lynn Henry brought out Charro, a ten-year-old thoroughbred cross Appaloosa mare, to show off her training for reporter Jane McDonald of *Yorkshire Today*. Without either a halter or a lead rope, Charro cantered gracefully around the outdoor circle, from time to time altering her pace by responding to voice and arm commands. Ms. Henry had but to point to a trailer, and the superbly trained Charro loaded herself into the vehicle as if she were preparing for transport.

Just a year ago, Lynn Henry explained to Jane McDonald, Charro would go on rampages, kicking, biting, rearing, and charging. The horse was considered so dangerous that Ms. Henry was seriously advised to sell the animal for dog food.

That was when Lynn Henry decided to try the Parelli system on Charro. Within months, Charro became a calm, well-disciplined, model horse. The system, she explained, is based on understanding animal behavior, using rewards, giving comfort, and using horse psychology to break the vicious circle of force, fear, and intimidation.

Bill Northern is a retired Virginia businessman, who used to deal in office supplies and race and breed horses on the side. In the late 1990s, he discovered his previously unknown talent as an "animal communicator" and began a new career serving as a kind of translator and arbitrator between owners and their pets. Northern, who spends winters on his ranch in New Zealand, appears to have a special gift for communicating with horses, and he has become a "horse whisperer" *par excellence.*

When Bill Northern talks to horses, they talk back to him. And he says that he hears them speak in complete sentences, with subjects, verbs, and adjectives. And horses sound different from each other, just as humans have their own personal peculiarities of speech. And horses sound very different from dogs and cats, speaking in a much more forceful manner.

In general, Northern observed, horses think that humans are around to provide services for them. If a horse's owner is late bringing its oats for dinner, the horse thinks, "What's wrong with so-and-so? Why is my meal late?" A dog in a similar situation thinks, "What have I done wrong to deserve a late meal? I'll try to do better." And a cat grouses, "The chow is late. I'm going to go kill something."

Most people who have owned horses have come to realize that their animals may be extremely sensitive and responsive to moods and emotions. Those individuals who have called upon Bill Northern for a consultation to help them better understand their horses have learned that their animals may possess very complex thoughts and emotions of their own. Sometimes a horse's complaint may be as simple as wanting to be a jumper, rather than a racer; requesting a more comfortable bit in its mouth; or suggesting more vitamins in its daily food rations. In other, more complicated cases, the horse may have deeper issues with its owner.

In one instance, a horse that was acting in a sullen, withdrawn manner told Northern that it was behaving that way because it didn't like the name that its owner had given it. The horse considered it demeaning. Northern asked the animal to suggest a new title. When the owner agreed to try the new moniker his horse had requested, he was amazed to see an immediate and positive change in the horse's behavior. The horse lifted its head proudly and responded at once to its new name.

In another case, a horse complained to Northern that its owner had cursed it and called it a bad name. Its feelings had been hurt, and it had been misbehaving ever since. Northern confronted the owner, who admitted that he had sworn at his horse several weeks earlier when he was riding some distance from the ranch. He apologized to the horse, and their relationship once again became harmonious.

A horse's pride tells it that it is smarter than its owner, Northern advises horse owners. "If he can understand you, and you can't understand him, he's probably correct."

Penelope Smith, author of *Animals: Our Return to Wholeness*, employs an ability that she calls "interspecies telepathic communication" in order to establish a meaningful connection between animals and their owners. In the May 1993 issue of *Fate* magazine, Penelope told how she had helped a horse named Chaca and her owner, Elaine, to find peace.

When Penelope first established telepathic communication with Chaca, she learned that the horse suffered from a disease of the bones in the feet and was no longer able to be ridden. Chaca was feeling depressed and useless to the point where she was not eating. Although Chaca knew Elaine still loved her and saw her daily, she felt worthless because she could no longer be ridden.

Penelope advised Elaine to obtain either another horse or some other animal to keep Chaca company. Elaine borrowed Charley, a mule, from a neighbor, and everything appeared to be going well—until the mule became cantankerous and started kicking at or chewing on trees, barns, fences, and even friend's automobiles. Once again, Elaine called Penelope for help.

When Penelope telepathically contacted Charley, the mule told her that he loved all the attention that he would receive when Elaine ran out to the pasture to scream at him for his latest misdeed. But when Penelope explained that he would be returned to his lonely pasture if he didn't stop his wanton destructive acts, Charley became morose. He was only acting up to get Elaine to respond to him as well as to Chaca.

Penelope instructed Elaine to let Charley know that he, too, was loved, but that he must behave and live in harmony with Chaca. Elaine took the animal communicator's advice, and when she next contacted Penelope, it was to report that the mare and the mule were romping happily and harmoniously in the pasture.

Many open-minded scientists believe firmly that there may be some kind of communication passing between animals and humans on an unconscious, intuitive level. However, nonverbal communication between humans and animals is a two-way street, and there seems little question that animals are much more sensitive to "reading" humans than people are to understanding the emotions or the needs of their pets or livestock. A dog, cat, or horse is generally extremely sensitive to a human's moods and unspoken feelings, which explains why some people have a much better instant rapport with animals than others.

Penelope Smith advises all prospective horse whisperers and other species communicators to practice love for the animal as acceptance, respect, reverence, goodwill, and a sincere recognition of the brotherhood/sisterhood of all living things. If people wish to establish a bond, a connection, with their animals, they must be certain that their expression of love is not contaminated by a condescending view of animals as underlings to be pitied. Smothering animals with excessive affection or attention can demean them and prevent them from being themselves and growing.

In *Animals: Our Return to Wholeness,* Penelope Smith warns that such a neurotic aspect of love "can make it impossible for people to accept their animal companions as independent agents—spirits who have their own feelings, thoughts, and responsibility for their own lives. . . . These people aren't quite able to consider that animals have minds of their own, or that they can make a telepathic connection with them."

Another stumbling block that many aspiring animal communicators encounter is that of their own doubt that they are able to receive telepathic messages from animals. Actually, Penelope suggests, if a person loves animals, he or she already "hears" what they are saying to some degree—even if they are not aware that they are receiving such communication.

Learning to listen to animals, Penelope Smith says, will enable the animal lover to better understand his or her fellow humans, as well. Such an acceptance of interspecies communication fosters an ability that ". . . boosts the understanding, joy, and richness possible in relationships with animal companions and all of life."

*T*he first settlers of the central Texas hill country in the 1820s were Scotch-Irish hillmen who had migrated from the states of Kentucky and Tennessee. God-fearing though they were, a vein of superstition and a healthy respect for the supernatural ran through their heritage. When advised by the local Comanche tribe to avoid a small valley because of a strange apparition that appeared on horseback, they told themselves there was enough land to go around without trespassing on haunted ground and they steered wide of the foreboding little hollow.

A few white men who had dared to get near enough to the place to hear anything said that they had heard mysterious sounds, like metal striking metal. But most reasonable folk wrote off the reports as tall tales and "injun spook stories."

One of the "reasonable" people who trespassed on haunted ground was a rancher named McConnell. A marauding pack of wolves had been tearing at his herd, and he tracked them to the draw that led into the hollow one day in 1846. Without hesitation, he pushed on into the little valley that had seldom supported the weight of a human being. After going about a hundred yards, he dismounted from his horse and bent near the ground to examine the confusing animal tracks more closely.

The clank of metal and the sounds of hooves caused him to snap up his head. He was astounded to see an armored rider thundering down the hollow. Terrified, he jumped on his own pony and galloped out of the place toward his house.

Shortly after the incident, the people of the hill country learned that the army of General Zachary Taylor had crossed the Rio Grande and had violated Mexican territory. The Mexican war had begun.

The Devil Rider of Chisholm Hollow is a strange manifestation that some of the people of the central Texas hills claim to have seen before every major conflict in which the United States has become embroiled. The strikingly tall, armored horseman on his magnificent, coal black steed is seen to thunder out of the little valley and make an appearance, then vanish without a trace.

The second recorded appearance of the rider was fifteen years after he had terrified McConnell. The report was given by Emmett Ringstaff, and this time the armored rider was more completely described.

On April 10, 1861, Ringstaff happened to be passing the hollow when the rider came by him at a steady trot. The horse he rode was taller than any that had been raised by the settlers of the area, and even though the country folk thought the rider to be a manifestation of Lucifer, Ringstaff remained calm enough to observe that the specter was wearing a particular kind of light armor and carrying a shield. Iron gauntlets covered his arms, and he wore a helmet of Spanish design. From a buckler, which looked to be gold and bore an inscription of a crown and a lion, two brass single barrel pistols dangled. The pistols were of eighteenth-century design and had the look of fine Spanish craftsmanship about them.

Shortly after Ringstaff saw the apparition of the rider, the first guns of the Civil War were fired at Fort Sumter.

After the war had ended, the haunted valley was christened Chisholm Hollow, because of its geographical location on a spur of the Chisholm trail, which Texas cattle owners used to drive their stock to Kansas railheads. Though the phantom horseman never seemed to bother the cattlemen, the cowboys did happen to pick up a few interesting articles out of the hollow, including a large silver spur that was Spanish in origin.

Still later, the settlers learned from historians that a Spanish fort had been located near the hollow when Texas had been under Spain's control. According to the historians, the garrison that had been stationed near the fort had been massacred by Comanche Indians around 1700.

Gradually, the theory that the rider was a manifestation of the devil gave way to the notion that he was the ghost of one of the Spaniards that had been killed in the massacre of almost two centuries before.

Before the Spanish-American war broke out in 1898, the mysterious rider was seen by three men—Arch Clawson, Ed Shannon, and Sam Bulluck. Although the pattern of the dark horseman's visitation had not changed, a new twist had been added. Each one of the men who saw the rider felt, at that particular instant, a weird flash of personal animosity that the rider directed at him. The phantom seemed to be sensitive about his Spanish heritage. Though the strange ghostly horseman had remained neutral when portending other conflicts, this time his loyalty was for Spain, and it seemed to be showing.

During the brief conflict with the European power, strange things happened around the central Texas hills. Though Texas had better than average rainfall in 1898, wells and creeks went dry in the hill country. Cattle died of thirst, and a strange and unexplainable disease began taking the horses. The local calamity is still blamed on the "dark devil rider" by some of the old-timers who live in the area of the hollow.

Only one attempt was ever made to settle the hollow, and that was unsuccessful. Scoffing at the superstitions of the small ranching community, a newcomer began building a house so he could claim homestead rights on the land in the hollow. He had just completed the structure when the entire building seemed to erupt in flames. It is said that all that has remained of the reckless effort is a crumbling chimney.

After his appearance before the Spanish-American war, the apparition seemed to keep to himself in the shadows of the secluded hollow. His next visitation was made in January of 1917 to a group of young deer hunters who were tempting the spooks by looking for deer signs within the hollow. Laughing at the wild tales of their elders, but glancing occasionally over their shoulders just the same, they had entered the hollow very cautiously. When the armored rider thundered out of nowhere, armor and mail glinting in the January sun, the young men scattered and ran. On February 3, 1917, the United States, which had been teetering on the brink of war, severed diplomatic relations with the German Empire and shortly after was sending armies across the Atlantic.

The world was hypertense in 1941. Europe had been a battlefield for two years, and the Western Pacific had been subject to Japanese aggression for even longer. Not insensitive to the precarious position of the United States in this world setting, the people of the central hill country of Texas had gathered to pray for peace on Sunday, December 7.

Following the services, two young couples got into an automobile and started down the road that led to Chisholm Hollow. When passing the haunted valley, the driver stopped the car, claiming that he had heard the sound of a horse. After a few seconds, the mounted apparition charged onto the road, stood broadside to them for an instant, then passed off the road and disappeared in the cover on the opposite side.

The terrified men and women hurried to one of the couples' homes, where they waited impatiently around the radio as the tubes warmed up. The first word they heard was of the bombing of Pearl Harbor.

There are those who swear that the Devil Horseman of Chisholm Hollow appeared before the Korean Conflict in 1950, during peaks of fighting throughout the hostilities in Vietnam from 1954 to 1975, and, more recently, before the Persian Gulf War in 1991. Others scoff and say that if the Dark Rider ever did exist, he has faded into the shadows of the past.

There were people who laughed out loud and hurled insults at Ruffian the first time that she appeared on a racetrack for the 5½-furlong event at Belmont on May 22, 1974. Raucous racing fans mocked the two-year-old filly as being too fat to compete with the other horses. Experienced betters howled that someone would have to be crazy to place a bet on Ruffian to win anything other than last place. Others thought it was the owners of such a fat freak who were crazy to place her at the starting gate with all the other fine-looking horses. A number of "experts" in the stands shared "inside" information that Ruffian's girth measured a chubby 75½ inches.

Imagine the shock and surprise of the mockers and the scoffers when the "fat freak" dominated the other horses from the time she left the starting gate and crossed the wire to finish by fifteen lengths.

Ruffian had tied the track record of 1:03 in her maiden race, and when she left the track, she appeared as though she had hardly broken a sweat. In fact, she looked as if she might be disappointed that the race was over or that she couldn't challenge all comers to another gallop around the track. Within a year of her debut, Ruffian had established herself as racing's greatest filly.

The nearly black foal came into the world at Claiborne Farm in Kentucky, born of some breeding stock owned by Mr. and Mrs. Stuart Janey for their Locust Hill Farm. Ruffian's sire was Reviewer; her dam was Shenanigans. In spite of Ruffian's being one of the largest foals to have been born on Claiborne Farm, her trainer, Frank Whitely Jr., recognized that she was something special. Once Ruffian got on the track with other horses, there was no holding her back.

After Ruffian won her initial race, she was moved up to stakes competition and she won the 5½-furlong Fashion Stakes at Belmont in the same record time of 1:03. Later that year at the Astoria Stakes at Aqueduct, she shaved a smidgeon off her own standard when she crossed the wire at 1:02 4/5.

In each race during her two-year-old season, Ruffian got faster. She won the six-furlong Sorority Stakes in July at 1:09, and she clocked in across the finish line at the Spinaway Stakes in Saratoga at 1:08 3/5,

breaking the previous records held by Man o' War
and Secretariat. No challenger could catch the big,
beautiful filly. She was no longer called the "fat freak."
She had a new nickname, "the Heartbreaker," because
of the speed with which she would pull away from all
the other horses in the pack and leave them several
lengths behind. No racing fan expressed any surprise
when Ruffian was named the champion juvenile filly
of 1974.

Ruffian's three-year-old season began with an
easy win on April 14, 1974, at the Caltha Purse at
Aqueduct. She went on to triumph at the Comely
Stakes, winning by 8½ lengths; the Acorn Stakes,
by 8¼ lengths; and the Mother Goose Stakes by 14
lengths.

The Acorn Stakes and the Mother Goose Stakes
serve as the first two legs of the American Filly Triple
Crown. By winning both of those races, Ruffian was
eligible for the Coaching Club American Oaks, the
third leg of the series. A crowd of over 30,000 racing
aficionados turned out to watch Ruffian win by 2¾
lengths.

On July 6, more than 50,000 racing enthusiasts
came to Belmont Park to watch a remarkable match
that had been arranged between the 1975 Derby winner, Foolish Pleasure, and Ruffian. The whole of the
racing world and millions of racing fans were curious

to see how the champion filly would do against the colt that had won the Derby. Jacinto Vasquez, the jockey who happened to be the regular rider for both Foolish Pleasure and Ruffian, chose the filly for the big race. Braulio Baeza was the rider for the Derby winner.

Foolish Pleasure left the starting gate to move past Ruffian by a head, but the filly quickly closed the gap and stuck her head out in front. Ruffian had increased her lead by about half a length as the two horses approached the turn. The crowd cheered wildly as the pair came down to the mile marker side by side.

And then, as both jockeys would later state, there was a terrible snapping sound, like that of a board breaking in half. Ruffian's off-fore sesamoid bones had shattered. The crowd that had been loudly cheering one of the most exciting races of the century was now struck silent in horror as it understood what had happened to racing's greatest filly.

As soon as he realized what had happened to Ruffian, Baeza slowed Foolish Pleasure to a canter. But Ruffian kept going. She knew her job was to race and to win. There was no stopping her. By the time Vasquez managed to pull her up, her hoof dangled uselessly. Still, in spite of what must have been excruciating pain, she had to be led off the track.

A team of four veterinarians and an orthopedic surgeon worked for twelve hours throughout the afternoon and into the night in an effort to save the life of the valiant Ruffian. Tragically, after the anesthesia wore off, a confused Ruffian awakened and began to thrash about, trying to get to her feet. Although several attendants attempted to hold her down, Ruffian broke the cast on her leg and caused further damage to her fetlock. Knowing that she was in awful pain and could not survive further surgery, the veterinarians put her down shortly after 2:00 A.M.

Hundreds of fans gathered to pay their last respects to the great racer when Ruffian was buried near the flagpole of Belmont Park, the site of her first triumph and her last race, which many experts believed she would have won if it were not for the accident. Although her career last only about thirteen months, Ruffian is almost always included on any racing buff's list of all-time great runners.

*I*rene Meadows told us that for a few years in the 1950s she and her mother lived on the farm in Kansas with her grandmother Bonnie Diedrich. Irene's father was stationed in South Korea with the army, and when Grandpa Diedrich passed away, her mother decided to move from Kansas City in order to keep Grandma company and to help them save on rent money.

Irene remembers those pastoral summers when she was eleven to thirteen years old as idyllic. Her mother, Opal, worked part-time in the pharmacy in town, and Irene would help her grandmother work in the large vegetable garden and feed the chickens and pigs. Because her grandmother was nearly deaf, Irene had to answer the telephone whenever it rang, and she loved the feeling that she was able to be

Grandma Bonnie's personal secretary.

Most of all, Irene recalls with delight the afternoons that she spent riding Casper, a spirited little Shetland pony. "I would ride Casper around the pasture, the barnyard, and sometimes over to Uncle Clay and Aunt Joyce's farm, about a mile away," Irene said. "I truly felt adventurous when I would set out on horseback all by myself and ride along the creek bank, through the woods, and then let Casper break into a trot on the gravel road that led to Aunt Joyce and her fresh-baked chocolate chip cookies."

Irene told us that little Casper had been named for Grandpa's cousin, who she was told was a small man, but very strong. "Casper was only about forty inches tall, but he was really a strong riding pony, and very gentle with children," she said. "Grandpa and Grandma used to have several horses, but Grandma sold them all except Casper when Grandpa died. Casper had become too much of a friend, she said, and besides, she teased me with a sly smile, if she hadn't kept Casper, then I would have had only Prince, their old collie, to ride to Aunt Joyce's."

One afternoon in July, eleven-year-old Irene climbed upon Casper, waved to her grandmother, and told Casper to "giddyap." Aunt Joyce had invited her to ride over that afternoon, and she would sew doll clothes with her.

Although Irene knew her grandmother was nearly deaf, she still shouted out her good-bye. "Grandma could see my lips moving, and so I waved and called good-bye again," she said. Then she and Casper started off at a fast trot on the trail to Aunt Joyce's.

The sky was cloudy and it was dark, although it was only a little past noon. That meant rain, and Irene hurried so that she would reach Aunt Joyce's before it started.

"Giddyap, Casper," said Irene, and the pony trotted faster. He knew the way to Aunt Joyce's as well as Irene did. He carefully negotiated the narrow trail along the creek bank, picked up speed on the wider path through the woods, then he turned in at the gate to Aunt Joyce's lane without even being told to or being given a slight touch of the reins.

"You're a smart pony," said Irene as she put Casper in the barn. "'You know the way to Aunt Joyce's and you know the way home again, too. You could take me home even if I were sound asleep."

Then she hurried into Aunt Joyce's big kitchen. "Here I am, Aunt Joyce," she said. "I've come to make doll clothes, just as we planned."

"Right you are," laughed Aunt Joyce as she finished fixing an apple pie and slipped it into the oven. "I'm glad old Casper got you here before it started to rain. The wind's coming up strong, too, and I don't like the looks of that black sky—one little bit."

Irene looked out at the sky. "I could see that clouds were gathering and that it was getting blacker, but I was more interested in sewing doll clothes than the weather. I asked Aunt Joyce if we could listen to music on the radio while we were sewing, and she said that would be all right, but she would choose the station. I knew it would be a country-western station, but I didn't mind, as long as we were making doll clothes."

Soon they were so busy sewing that Aunt Joyce forgot her concerns about the weather. Suddenly the music on the radio stopped and the announcer's voice said, "Tornado warning! There could be a twister headed this way. Get your chickens, cows, and other livestock under cover as soon as possible—and then grab your family and head for shelter. Fasten everything down if you don't want it to blow away—including yourselves!"

Aunt Joyce didn't wait to hear the rest. She jumped up, grabbed Irene's hand, and said they had to make a quick check on the livestock before they headed for the storm cellar in back of the house. Aunt Joyce kept saying over and over that she wished Uncle Clay were home, but he had gone to a nearby town on business and she knew he would take shelter there.

Irene was helping Aunt Joyce shoo the chickens into the hen house when she suddenly clapped
her hand over her mouth in dismay. "Grandma!" I
exclaimed. "Grandma's all alone and can't hear the
radio. She won't know the tornado is on its way!"

"Let's try the telephone—quick!" said Aunt
Joyce, and they rushed back to the house.

Aunt Joyce let the telephone ring and ring, but
Grandma didn't answer.

Irene said that she would have to go and tell her,
but Aunt Joyce wouldn't even think of letting her go
with a tornado on the way.

"Your Grandmother's weather-wise," Aunt Joyce
said. "She'll know a big storm or tornado is coming if
she looks at the sky."

"But what if she should be taking her nap and
won't see the sky?" Irene said. "What can we do?"

"If only we had someone to send," Aunt Joyce
said. "I'm too big to ride Casper and I'd never make it
in time just walking."

Suddenly Irene sprang to her feet with the obvious solution. "We do have someone to send," she
said. "We can send Casper. He knows the way home
as well as I do. He'll go home if I tell him to. Write a
note, Aunt Joyce. Quick."

"Of course!" agreed Aunt Joyce, and she hastily
scribbled the storm warning on a piece of paper and

added that Irene would stay there until the storm was over and the possible tornado had passed.

It took only a minute to fasten the note to Casper's saddle.

"Go home, Casper," Irene told the Shetland. "Home! Home!"

Irene said that she remembers giving Casper a little slap on his flank, and he started off down the lane. Casper was weather-wise, too. He knew that a storm was coming, and so he hurried to get home to his own stable in the warm barn.

Before he was more than halfway home, the rain came, soaking the pony to the skin. The lightning flashed and thunder rumbled, and a strong wind began to howl and bend the branches of the trees that arched over the trail through the woods.

"I watched Casper until he was out of sight and Aunt Joyce made me go down into the storm cellar with her," Irene said.

Later, they learned that Grandma Bonnie had been awakened from her nap by the roar of the powerful wind as it billowed the curtains in front of the open windows in the living room and knocked over a vase. She took one look at the dark and ominous sky and began to worry about Irene. She prayed that she would not try to beat the storm and leave Aunt Joyce's for home.

When she looked out the east window toward the woods, she was panic-stricken when she saw a riderless Casper making his way along the trail. Grandma Bonnie had to fight back terrible thoughts of Irene being somehow thrown from the saddle and Casper coming home alone.

But then reason calmed her terror. She knew that Casper would never leave Irene injured on the trail. He would stay by her side if the Devil himself tried to frighten him away.

Suddenly, as Grandma Bonnie watched out the window in the front room, she saw lightning strike a tree along the woodland trail. Down it fell, crashing across the road in front of Casper. The startled Shetland reared up on his hind legs and snorted, but when nothing more happened, he calmed down. He walked skittishly around the tree, keeping one eye on it to see if it moved or posed any further threat, then he continued along the trail in the pouring rain.

Grandma Bonnie put a shawl over her head and met Casper when he arrived at the barn. Even if her hearing was still perfect, she would have been unable to hear him whinny above the howling wind, but she knew that Casper was calling for someone to give him clean hay and rub him dry.

"When she read the note that Aunt Joyce has fastened to Casper's saddle, Grandma Bonnie told us that she had hugged the pony tight," Irene said. "Then she rubbed him dry, gave him clean hay and some oats besides, and told him how brave and smart he was."

Her grandmother also said that she had given thanks to the Lord that Irene was all right, then she kept on rubbing Casper and told him, "You can't fit in the storm cellar with me, old friend, and I'm not leaving you out here alone to face a tornado. If the good Lord decrees it to be our time, we'll just have to go together. We know we have a lot of good folks who'll be greeting us on the other side."

Irene Meadows concluded her story by saying that although the strong storm winds tore the roof off the barn and destroyed a couple of outbuildings, the good Lord turned the tornado aside that day. Grandma Bonnie did not meet the good folks waiting for her on the other side until 1974, when she died at the age of eighty-seven. Casper had gone to the green pastures in the sky in 1973, at the age of thirty-five, so the family knew that Grandma had ridden into glory on the back of the trusty little Shetland pony.

*C*ivil War historians estimate that military personnel rode approximately 100,000 horses into battle and that another 1.5 million horses were employed as draft animals, transporting supply wagons, ammunition carts, and cannons from the site of one conflict to another. An analysis of war records reveals that the average life span of a horse pressed into either cavalry service or supply hauling was about six months.

General U.S. Grant and Cincinnati

General Ulysses S. Grant, commanding general of the Union forces, entered the conflict as a colonel of the Twenty-first Illinois Volunteer Infantry on the back of a horse named Methuselah that he had purchased in Galena, Illinois. While the regiment was encamped in Springfield, he acquired a cream-colored stallion called Jack from a local farmer. Grant rode Jack until after the battle of Chattanooga in November 1863, but he continued to keep him for parades and ceremonial occasions, for he valued the horse as a handsome, noble, and intelligent animal.

Grant had a horse shot out from under him during the battle of Belmont on November 7, 1861, and he took the pony his son, Frederick Dent Grant, was riding. Later in the siege, Grant took the larger horse of Captain Hyllier, one of his aides-de-camp, and Frederick's pony was lost in the battle.

Fox, a powerful roan with great endurance, was Grant's mount for the battles around Fort Donelson and Shiloh. After the battle at Shiloh, Grant claimed a rawboned horse left behind by the Confederates. Although the animal was given the name Kangaroo by his troops because of its unusual appearance, Grant found it to be a very reliable and worthy horse after he had fed it and treated it well. The general used Kangaroo during the Vicksburg campaign and kept it until he switched to an easier-riding pony named Jeff Davis, so-called as a kind of ironic joke because it had been taken from the plantation of Joe, the brother of Jefferson Davis, president of the Confederacy.

General Grant's battle charger until the end of the war was Cincinnati, a son of the famous thoroughbred Lexington, at that time the fastest racehorse in the United States. Shortly after the horse was presented to him in 1864, Grant acclaimed Cincinnati as the finest horse that he had ever owned, and he was very particular about allowing anyone else to sit in the thoroughbred's saddle. It is said that he made only two exceptions—his lifelong friend Admiral David Ammen, who had saved Grant from drowning when they were boys, and President Abraham Lincoln.

General Robert E. Lee and Traveller

Another steed with the original name of Jeff Davis became the most famous horse in the Confederacy and one of the most well-known animals in the Civil War, South or North. As a colt, Jeff Davis won first prize in a race at the Lewisburg, Virginia, fair, and he was purchased by Major Thomas L. Broun. In the spring of 1862, when Major Broun observed how taken General Robert E. Lee seemed by the horse, he sold Jeff Davis to him for $200.

At the time of Lee's purchase, the stallion was five years old; stood about five feet three inches high; had a muscular, deep chest; and was gray, with a long mane and a flowing tail. Lee deemed the name "Jeff Davis" for a horse to be somewhat disrespectful to the president of the Confederacy, so he renamed the stallion Traveller, and it became his favorite charger throughout the campaign.

As it might be supposed, General Lee had other battle horses during the course of the war. For two years, he rode Lucy Long in alternation with Traveller. Lucy Long had been presented to him by General Jeb Stuart, and the horse was second only to Traveller in Lee's affection. Sadly, Lucy Long broke down under the stress of battle, as did his alternate horses Richmond, Ajax, and Brown Roan. Only Traveller withstood the hardships and rigors of constant warfare.

When Lee rode to Appomattox Court House on April 9, 1865, to accept the terms of surrender offered by the Union, he sat astride Traveller, and it was that same faithful gray stallion that the great Southern leader rode back to his army and then home to Richmond. Traveller remained with Lee when he became a private citizen and assumed the presidency of Washington and Lee University.

Such was Traveller's fame that a book was written purporting to be authored by the very mighty charger that Lee had ridden into battle on so many fierce occasions. The unique work that Traveller allegedly "dictated" to a ghost writer depicted the Civil War through the eyes of a horse and became very popular.

In 1866, the general's beloved Lucy Long was found and brought to Lexington to spend her last days with Traveller and the man whom she had served so well in battle. In 1870, when Robert E. Lee was carried to his final resting place, Traveller marched slowly beside the hearse, his head bowed, as if fully cognizant of the meaning of the somber occasion.

Traveller died in 1872, and his skeleton was on display at Washington and Lee University until May 8, 1971, when the remains were interred outside the Lee Chapel at the University, near the Lee family crypt.

General Philip H. Sheridan and Winchester

General Philip Sheridan's war horse was presented to him by officers in the Second Michigan Cavalry in Rienzi, Mississippi, in 1862. Sheridan named the horse Rienzi, and he rode the stalwart animal in nearly every engagement in which he participated throughout the duration of the Civil War. Rienzi was renamed Winchester after Sheridan made the famous ride on October 19, 1862, from Winchester to Cedar Creek, Virginia, in time to rally his troops and turn almost certain defeat into a victory for the Union. The dramatic incident was immortalized by Thomas Buchanan Read in his poem, "Sheridan's Ride." Winchester's mounted body is on display at the Hall of Armed Forces History, National Museum of American History, Smithsonian Institution, Washington, D.C.

General Jeb Stuart and Highfly

The dashing General James Ewell Brown (Jeb) Stuart's favorite charger was Highfly. Stuart rode the big and speedy bay through many battles and a number of very close calls. One of those narrow squeaks in which Stuart relied on the speed of his faithful horse has become legendary.

In the summer of 1862, while he was awaiting a rendezvous with General Fitzhugh Lee at Verdiersville, Stuart took off his signature black-plumed hat and stretched out for a siesta on a bench in front of a tavern. A bit later, hearing horses' hooves on the old plank road, Stuart roused himself and walked to the road anticipating the arrival of Fitzhugh Lee. To his great surprise and alarm, he met a number of Federal cavalry coming around the bend. Although Highfly was grazing unbridled in the yard near the tavern, Stuart managed to sprint for his horse, jump into the saddle, and leave the frustrated Union cavalrymen far behind him. He also left the black-plumed hat on the bench, but it was far better for the Confederacy that the Federal troops capture Stuart's trademark hat than the general himself.

General George G. Meade and Baldy

General George G. Meade's staff officers might have complained about the irregular pace and various idiosyncrasies of their commanding officer's horse, but Baldy proved to be an indestructible iron horse. The big bay horse with white face and feet was wounded twice at the first battle of Bull Run and was left for dead on the field at Antietam. Later, Federal troops found him grazing on the battleground, a deep gash in his neck.

Baldy recovered from his wounds and carried General Meade into battle at Fredericksburg and Chancellorsville. Two days into the fierce fighting at Gettysburg, Baldy was felled with a bullet that lodged between his ribs. Still, the valiant horse got to his feet, bloody and torn, but not defeated. Meade would not allow anyone to put Baldy down, but the severely wounded horse was removed from combat and sent to pasture at Dowingtown, Pennsylvania.

After the surrender of the Confederate Army at Appomattox, Meade traveled to Philadelphia to check on the health of his faithful charger. He was delighted to find Baldy fully recovered from his wounds. General Meade and his bullet-scarred war horse remained inseparable companions, and Baldy morosely followed the hearse to the cemetery when his master died in 1872. The gallant charger died ten years later, and Baldy's mounted head and fore hooves serve as respected reminders of his bravery at the George G. Meade Post, Grand Army of the Republic, in Philadelphia.

General Stonewall Jackson and Little Sorrel

When a Union officer's mount was captured by Confederate soldiers after the battle at Harpers Ferry, General Thomas Johnson "Stonewall" Jackson acquired the mare and presented it to his wife. Jackson named the horse Fancy, and returned to the army of the Confederacy riding his horse, Big Sorrel. Unfortunately, Big Sorrel was not the charger that a fighting general like Stonewall Jackson required. Although the mare that he had given his wife was about eleven years old, he commandeered Fancy, renamed her Little Sorrel, and hoped that she would prove to be more reliable in battle. Little Sorrel had heart, but she was so small that Jackson's feet nearly dragged on the ground.

In 1863, at the battle of Chancellorsville, Jackson was mounted on Little Sorrel when he fell under friendly fire from his own men and was mortally wounded. After the general's death, Little Sorrel was sent home to pasture at Mrs. Jackson's home in North Carolina. Later, to honor the memory of Jackson, Little Sorrel was presented as the mascot for the cadets at the Virginia Military Institute, where the general had taught. A few years after the end of the war, Little Sorrel was in great demand to be shown at fairs and exhibitions throughout the South. In 1886, Little Sorrel died at the age of thirty-six when she fell and broke her back.

"We didn't know what we had gotten ourselves into," said Colleen Steffanson in her letter to us, as she described what she called a "near mare nightmare."

Colleen explained, "My husband, Brian, and I had decided long ago that it would be wonderful to own horses *someday*—although our children insist that they were the ones with the idea."

After they had taken a large risk in buying an acreage in Montana, the Steffansons didn't have a penny to spare, but it was certain that ten-year-old Tammy and twelve-year-old Amy weren't in accord with waiting for a more secure financial time such as *someday*. "All the kids ever talked about was how much they wanted horses to complete the setting," Colleen said. "Brian and I thought they would grow weary of begging and settle for the many farm cats and a puppy, but after seven months of their persisting, we began putting our heads together for a creative solution."

Night after night, Brian and Colleen sat up going over the bills and thinking of the long-term commitment of feeding and caring for a horse, to say nothing of how much one would cost to buy. Although the old barn on the property truly looked destined to have several horses filling its stalls, what if they were to go out on a limb financially for a horse only to have it lose its luster when the kids discovered how much time and care it would take?

While watching an episode of Home and Garden TV's *Trash to Treasure* show, an inspiration hit Colleen. She wondered if someone might actually *want* to get rid of a horse that was no longer serving them—put it out to pasture, so to speak. The show's motto, "One person's trash is another's treasure" echoed in her mind and she decided to go for it. Not that any horse should be considered as trash, she rationalized, but certainly there must be some that for one reason or another are out of their prime as show horses, racehorses, workhorses, or even pets.

Colleen called the local newspapers and placed the following simple ad: **"WANTED: A horse to love . . . even if it has been put out to pasture!"**

After several weeks, someone called the newspaper for the phone number of whoever placed the ad and then called the Steffanson home with the information. Colleen had decided it best to handle the ad in such a manner, so if by chance someone did respond, she could screen any information to prevent premature enthusiasm over something that might not work out. Making sure there weren't any little listening ears nearby, she called the number given her just as Brian was walking in the door from work.

Motioning to him to come toward the phone, she scribbled on some paper what the call was about. After getting the details on the situation from the owner of the horse, she said she would call him back after discussing it with her husband. Colleen had of course mentioned her idea of placing the ad to Brian, but he didn't think anything would come of it.

"That was 'Jesse'—the only name we need to know, he said." Colleen smiled. "Says he has a horse that isn't much good for anything and that it's just as well with him if she were out of sight."

Jesse had sounded so gruff about the horse that a puzzled Colleen was reluctant even to consider it, but "free" was the right price and in reiterating the details she suddenly felt heartbroken that the horse was so unwanted.

They agreed sight unseen to take the horse and called Jesse to make the arrangements. Then they sat down with the girls and told them the exciting news, making it clear that the horse was fairly old, not a pony by any means, but that it needed a good family to give it love and care. Brian and Colleen emphasized the importance of making a commitment in adopting such a horse. The kids could hardly contain their squeals, nearly knocking mommy and daddy to the floor with a flying leap and hugs so hardy and spirited as to be nearly bruising.

Tammy and Amy came right home from school the next day so they could spend some extra time getting the barn ready for their dream horse. As they were stringing a big welcome sign, which they had colored in big letters, across the barn, they heard the sound of a truck turning onto the gravel road that led to their farm.

An old pickup, pulling a battered horse trailer, driven by a man looking equally as worn and weathered, slowly came to a stop, leaving a trail of dust in its wake. The Steffansons gathered to see old Jesse emerge from his squeaky, bent truck door. Without further ado, he headed straight for the back gate of the horse trailer.

Brian stepped forward, holding out his hand in greeting, but Jesse didn't so much as make eye contact or mumble words of introduction. He ignored Brian's outstretched hand as he said bluntly, "So you say you want a horse, do ya? Well here she is, just as I said."

The Steffansons all looked at each other in dismay at his strange behavior and uncivil manner. Old

Jesse opened the trailer door, grabbed a rope that was tied around the horse's collar, and yanked on the animal until she was out. "Don't have much more to tell about her other than what I told you on the phone," Jesse grumbled. "She's a twenty-year-old horse that won't do much of nothin', so good luck with her."

Jesse started to climb back into his pickup when he turned and pointed at the horse trailer. He offered to give them the old trailer, too, stating he had no need of it now. As he unhitched the trailer from his truck, he gazed at Brian holding the rope, which was also gripped by each of the kids. His tone softened slightly as he climbed into his truck. "Good luck to y'all," he mumbled as he started his engine and backed up away from the group, at least careful not to blaze a trail of dust behind him.

Colleen confessed that they all stood outside the barn nearly speechless as they tried to make sense out of their benefactor's strange manner and of the less-than-perfect vision of the horse that stood before them. Before the horse arrived, Amy and Tammy had already decided to name the horse Beauty—no matter what it looked like or what name it had been given before. But it was readily apparent that this was no beauty standing before them. It was, in fact, one of the ugliest horses they had ever seen.

Skinny, shaggy, mangy, dirty, and full of cockleburs, the horse was a sight to behold. The skeleton frame was poking out of what little flesh there was to cover it, and even that had open wounds punctuated by limbs swollen from neglect and malnutrition. How could the horse even be still alive they wondered.

Once they recovered somewhat from the initial shock and disappointment, compassion set in, and one by one, each of the Steffanson family expressed how badly they felt that the poor horse had been so mistreated and abused.

Not certain as to how to proceed, Brian thought it best to enlist the help of a veterinarian. Describing the horse's condition on the phone made them all suspect the horse might be so near death that it would be cruel to keep her alive, but the vet said the best they could do until he could arrive in several days would be to make it as comfortable as possible.

The family decided its name should still be Beauty, and they showered the mare with attention. The girls continually repeated, "Poor, poor, pooooor horsie," as they gingerly tried petting and stroking her tattered, filthy muzzle and sides. Daddy had already warned the girls the horse might not welcome their advances, so they were careful and gentle as they led the horse through a pasture and then to the barn and its stall.

Brian felt it certain that in addition to sheer neglect the old horse may have suffered beatings, so he and Colleen were slightly leery of how they should proceed. Regardless of the groundwork that they had lain with the girls regarding commitment and sticking with the decision to take on this responsibility, perhaps the best thing would be to turn over the horse to the vet, and let the vet offer a prognosis. They decided they should all sleep on it and talk about it after some prayers and thought.

The next morning upon arising, Colleen and Brian were panicked when they discovered that the girls were not in their room. They raced out to the barn to behold a marvelous sight.

Amy was standing on Mom's kitchen stepladder that she had dragged out to the barn, and Tammy, in soapy, soaked pajamas, was standing on an old orange crate. Washing their Beauty with a bucket of warm water with bubble bath in it and a bath sponge, the girls had never before displayed such affection for any of their pets, nor had they ever looked happier doing anything than at this very moment with this newfound friend.

The girls were so intent on what they were doing, they didn't even notice Mom and Dad were there, but when they looked up and saw their parents standing watching them, they saw tears in their parents' eyes.

Misinterpreting her parents' tears for disapproval, Amy blurted out, "Oh, please, Mommy and Daddy, don't take Beauty away from us. She needs soooo much love and we are going to fix her all up pretty and give her all the love she never got!"

Tammy added, "It wasn't her fault she didn't have a good family to take care of her like we can . . . please, please!"

"We knew right then, we couldn't say no," Colleen said. "Beauty soaked up every bit of love the girls gave her. Although slightly timid and weak, her manner was mild and even seemed appreciative of the newfound glory. A voracious appetite was the best sign, according to the vet. After examining Beauty, and prescribing several ointments and salves for the wounds and supplemental vitamins to add to her high-protein diet, he expressed his opinion that the horse could still have many good years left with the proper care.

Colleen believes that it was a divinely inspired idea to place that ad in the paper that brought Beauty into their family. Some of the most fundamental spiritual and emotional teachings came through to Amy and Tammy in a firsthand, hands-on way that may never have been possible at such depth by any other means. The girls didn't lose their motivation in caring for their gift horse.

Without being reminded, they spent nearly every waking moment that they weren't in school with their Beauty. They often even did their homework in the barn—or if the weather permitted, near her, with a table set up, so she could watch them as she grazed in the pasture. They curried her, fed her, washed her, talked to her, and occasionally sang and danced for her. Certainly, they learned responsibility.

But far outweighing the consistency of their discipline in caring for the horse came a life-teaching of compassion and looking beyond appearances. That old saying *"Beauty is only skin deep"* turned out to be more than relevant—not only in reference to their Beauty but also in their perceptions of their classmates and life around them.

"Tammy and Amy were at first dismayed when their friends teased them about such an ugly old mare," Colleen said. "They were saddened when their classmates would laugh and poke fun at Beauty. We had many discussions about how some of the kids at school carried the same attitude toward other classmates they thought 'ugly' or 'uncool.'"

The girls realized the importance of looking past outer appearances and of what a vast difference love and care can make—even on something or someone that seemed ugly or worthless to someone else. They watched as their Beauty filled out in form, gained in strength, and became one of their best friends in life.

Although Beauty's health had been restored, she never was what most people consider a *beautiful* horse, Colleen admitted. "Perhaps because of this, we experienced one of the greatest miracles: the discovery that there is a beauty of the soul that supercedes outer appearances. It carried over in each of our lives. The girls each befriended classmates at school who were ignored or picked on, and they were first to point out to the scoffers, teasers, and abusers how unfair they were behaving. Tammy and Amy set quite an example for many others as they discovered an unbreakable bond between them and their ugly horse named Beauty—and they continue to do so."

Brian and Colleen expressed that they, too, found themselves looking deeper into others' hearts and lives, rather than paying special attention to what they wore or what they looked like. "We were constantly reminded through our experience with Beauty that not all people—or animals—have the same opportunities or good fortune," Colleen said. "Many are beset with misfortune and sadness. But one thing is for certain: We *all* respond best to love and care."

Colleen says it has been five years since Beauty arrived in their lives. The girls have been able to ride her—at a very slow pace—but mainly, Beauty just "hangs around."

"She's the gentlest, kindest, most loving—and beautiful—horse that we could ever have," Colleen concluded.

As early as 1905, in an article for the August issue of *Annales des sciences psychiques*, M. Ernest Bozzano collected sixty-nine cases in which cats, dogs, and horses plainly gave evidence that they perceived, often before humans did, apparitions and phantasms of the dead. Bozzano noted that horses in particular seem very sensitive "to places that pass as haunted or uncanny."

In the October 25, 2002, issue of the *Shropshire Star*, Perkin Bosworth, from Mill Farm in Hughley, Shropshire, U.K., said that his horses detect ghostly spirits each time they are made to cross a haunted ford. Each time the horses are ridden to the haunted bridge near Hughley, they halt, hesitant to cross over it.

Bosworth sensed that Truffle and the other horses were picking up some paranormal link with the past. Perhaps some dramatic event of long ago could still be perceived by sensitive people and animals who passed through Harnage Ford. The farm owner had always respected his horses as being very intelligent animals. Perhaps they had a highly developed sixth sense.

Bosworth researched the history of Harnage Ford and discovered a long-ago tragedy that might be influencing his sensitive horses. In the early 1800s, the squire who lived at Harnage Grange was traveling to Langley Chapel in a carriage with his daughter on her wedding day, when the horses suddenly bolted on their approach to Harnage Ford. Inexplicably, the horses ran down the ford and turned the carriage over. One of the horses drowned, and the bride-to-be was thrown. She died when she struck her head on some rocks near the riverbank. Only the sorrowful squire survived.

Somehow, Bosworth speculates, his horses have a psychic ability that enables them to receive impressions of the skittish carriage horses and the accident they caused that cost a young bride her life over 200 years ago. For a few moments, the horses from Mill Farm hesitate at the bridge, reluctant to cross it until they are able to separate the present from the phantoms of the past.

*I*n her public lectures, Samantha Khury, a psychic sensitive from Manhattan Beach, California, encourages all pet owners to communicate with their animals through "mental imagery." The key, she says, whether one wishes to become a "horse whisperer" or to have a better understanding of one's pet, is to concentrate on the animal and think about its daily actions and habits. If the horse practices a habit that you would like to correct, visualize it acting the way you want it to do. Soon the horse will begin to pick up the mental picture of your desire—and it will obey.

One of the most famous of the early real-life "Dr. Doolittles" was a man named Fred Kimball, who definitely seemed to talk to the animals and to be able to understand them when they talked back. Meeting Kimball in Los Angeles some years back was a unique experience, and we remember him as a gentle, white-haired man who presented a strong image of frank sincerity.

A former wrestler, Marine jujitsu instructor, sharpshooter, champion swimmer, and merchant seaman, Kimball recalled his days many years ago with the Army Engineers in Panama, chopping roads through the heavy jungle. Kimball stated that anyone can develop his or her senses and intuition to a higher degree to learn to communicate with animals. "The simple man finds his way out of the woods while the scholar gets lost," he said. "The intellectual needs to listen more to his heart."

Kimball illustrated an extremely pragmatic by-product of being able to "talk" to the animals. Once a friend in Florida needed some money in order to get married. Kimball talked to the horses at the Hialeah racetrack and picked fourteen winners out of the seventeen races.

"You can't always win them all," he said, shrugging off the three losses. "The horse may be on the level, but it may not have a good rider."

Kimball said that horses are able to store up vast memory banks and that it was this information that he tapped. He claimed that it is not difficult to speak with dogs, because they use basic terms. When he communicated with canines, Kimball said that he used symbols to learn their problems and complaints.

"Dogs often complain because their masters do not demand enough of them," he stated. "Dogs like to be trained and active. Some even become a bit bored with their human family."

"I don't really *talk* to them," Kimball explained, referring to his oft-demonstrated ability to calm and apparently communicate with troubled domestic and wild animals. "I focus on their minds with mental telepathy. The animal has in its memory certain things that the owner may have forgotten. The animal gives me a mental picture of what it wants to say and then I 'translate' it for people. The language of animals is very much like the language of children."

In Kimball's worldview, modern men and women simply do not ask enough of Mother Nature. "The divine nature knocks gently at the door of your consciousness and does not force itself upon you. If one is not receptive or refuses to open the door, this divine nature recedes. Many people shut out a great deal from their lives because of their conventional fears."

Becoming One with Nature

Here is an exercise that can help you to grow in greater balance with nature and to walk in greater harmony with Mother Earth. You might try it the next time that you are walking with your horse in the woods, the beach, the desert, or in a city park.

Take a comfortably deep breath, hold it for the count of three, then release it. Repeat this three times.

Look toward the North. Let your eyes go to the far, far horizon of the North. Feel yourself growing as you look toward the North.

Visualize yourself stretching upward, as if you were a tree. Stretch your arms out in front of you as if they were tree limbs stretching forth.

Imagine that you can touch the far horizon of the North. Then, turning slowly, imagine that your arms stretch out and touch the horizon, the great pole of the horizon. Feel your fingertips touching the very farthest reaches of the horizon as you begin to move slowly around in a counterclockwise circle.

Perhaps your fingertips touch a mountaintop . . . a cloud . . . an ocean wave . . . the shoreline of a lake . . . the rolling grasses of a plain. Wherever you touch, as you move slowly with your arms stretching from horizon to horizon, let Mother Earth know that you are aware of her energy. Bless her and all that you touch. Ask Mother Earth to bless you and your horse. Ask Mother Earth to guide the two of you to walk together in harmony, peace, and love.

Keep your eyes open as you move counterclockwise. Feel your fingertips brush the farthest reaches that you can see with your eyes.

Now close your eyes and know that you and your horse are focal points for energies from a higher source. There is Mother Earth all around you. There are the heavenly energies above you. And all around you are the seen and unseen energies of the Great Mystery.

You, through your mind, constitute the focal point that touches the Universe, that caresses Mother Earth. Open all of your senses to receive the blessing that Mother Earth sends back to you.

Feel yourself and the spirit essence of your horse blending together and becoming One with All That Is. Feel and know that the two of you have become the center of a great benevolent energy that is consecrated by all that surrounds you.

Developing a Harmonious State of Oneness with Your Horse

Sit quietly with your horse in a place where you will be undisturbed for at least thirty minutes. Calm yourself and attempt to clear your mind of all negative and troublesome thoughts.

Take a comfortably deep breath, hold it for the count of three, then exhale slowly. Repeat this procedure three times.

Begin to focus on the thought that you and your horse are one in mind and spirit. Form a mental picture of the two of you in perfect harmony.

This mental picture must make no reference to any of your horse's negative habits. This ideal picture must not contain any image of any aspect of your horse's behavior that you might wish to modify or change. You must focus only on that ideal image of the two of you in perfect harmony and in a complete loving relationship. You must believe with all your soul essence that you are now living in the perfect blending of Oneness.

Once you have fashioned the image of you and your horse melding perfectly into a Oneness of mind and spirit, hold that picture fast and begin to inhale very slowly, taking comfortably deep breaths.

As you inhale, you are drawing in what the mystics refer to as the *mana* or the *prana* and what martial artists refer to as the *ki* or *chi*, the all-pervasive life force. This is the energy of miracles, and it will permit you to shape the ideal condition of Oneness with your horse.

Create and hold fast in your mind the picture of your perfect Oneness with your horse as you inhale and draw in the *mana*. The *mana* will give the image enough strength to hold together while your soul begins to materialize the picture into physical actuality.

Hold the picture firmly in your mind and continue to breathe slowly, sending vital energy to your soul.

Be alive in the picture.

Feel it.

Keep your mind from all negative thoughts and permit the perfect harmony of complete Oneness with your horse to continue to grow. Once you work steadily at achieving a Oneness with your horse, you will enter a beautiful realm of understanding in which you will see very clearly that the strange powers of horses manifest most profoundly in the energy of love that we two-leggeds have always the choice of sharing with our brothers and sisters among the four-leggeds, the winged ones, the beings that crawl on their bellies, and the creatures who live in the waters. Once we learn to express respect rather than condescension, and love rather than ownership, we, too, shall greatly expand our own powers of spirit.

Exercises to Establish Telepathic Communication with Your Horse

Here is a very simple exercise to help you develop a closer telepathic bond with your horse. Telepathy is an ability that we all have and that is quite easy to trigger. All you need to do to make contact with your horse is to think intently of it and form a mental image of what you wish to communicate.

Think of the mind as a vast reservoir of energy ready to be released into the unknown. Form the image in your mind, then let go of it and visualize it floating into your horse's brain.

As a gauge of your success in this exercise, you should set a time limit on your thought projection, then note how long it takes to get a positive feedback or response.

You might start by mentally asking your horse to come to you when you are in different outdoor areas. Keep projecting the thought until your horse responds to the unspoken command.

On another occasion, wait until your horse has its back turned toward you and is comfortably relaxing or focusing on some other activity. Begin to concentrate on the back of the animal's head.

Imagine that there is a stream of light flowing from your eyes. Then imagine that on that stream of light you are sending the message, "Turn around and look at me. Now come to me."

Don't be discouraged if your horse does not turn around and look at you immediately. Just keep at it, and within a few minutes your horse will turn and stare directly at you and heed your unspoken summons to join you.

You should never keep at these exercises until you are weary of them or bored. You must always maintain a fresh, enthusiastic attitude for best results.

After some practice, the results you will achieve will be quite dramatic, and you will have progressed much further toward establishing a powerful telepathic link with your horse.

*M*ost of us tend to think of horseback riding as a pleasure sport enjoyed by the young, nimble, and able-bodied, but there is a rapidly growing worldwide movement gaining in popularity and success in the use of horses as a phenomenal form of therapy for the disabled. *Hippotherapy* (from the Greek root word "hippo" for "horse"), as it has come to be called, is the use of the horse as therapist, and the technique has developed into an internationally established physical therapy practice in the medical and educational fields. Teachers, speech therapists, occupational and physical therapists, psychiatrists, and other medical doctors all refer students and patients to riding programs. Horses are helping those humans who refuse to allow their disabilities to rule their lives to rise far above their infirmities to a new-found freedom of movement and skill.

The concept is not entirely new. More than 2,000 years ago, history records that the ancient Greeks used horseback riding as therapy for people with disabilities. In 600 B.C., Orbasis of ancient Lydia documented that the value of horses was not limited to being an excellent means of transportation, but that horses were found to improve the health and well-being of those who had various mental and physical handicaps.

In 460–377 B.C., followers of Hippocrates established horseback riding as a panacea for a great variety of maladies, recommending it as a preferred treatment. Thomas Sydenham (1624–1689), the seventeenth-century physician who was known as the "English Hippocrates," stated that horseback riding was preferable to all other exercises.

One of the earliest actual studies of horseback riding as therapy dates back to 1875. After using riding as a treatment for patients with a variety of problems, Cassaign, a French physician, was convinced of the value of horse therapy. Cassaign documented vast improvement in certain kinds of neurological disorders by improving his patients' balance, posture, joint movement, and all-around psychological strength.

In 1946, Scandinavia was hit with several devastating outbreaks of poliomyelitis. Among the many afflicted was a very accomplished horsewoman named Lis Hartel. Able to walk with crutches after undergoing extensive surgical and physiotherapy treatments, she was bravely determined to ride again. Her daily persistence in supervised riding sessions resulted in remarkable improvement in her coordination and muscle strength and led her to win the silver medal for dressage (guiding a horse through a series of complex maneuvers by slight movements of the rider's weight, legs, and hands) in the Helsinki 1952 Olympic Games, which, in turn, gained more worldwide attention for horseback riding as therapeutic. Copenhagen physical therapist Ulla Harpoth and Lis Hartel applied what they learned firsthand and went on to develop the use of horses as a miraculous therapy for other patients.

In England, Oxford Hospital used riding therapy for British soldiers who were wounded in World War I. Encouraged with the successful results, in the 1950s they explored its use for all types of handicaps. The findings were so beneficial, they resulted in the 1969 establishment of the British Riding for the Disabled Association (RDA)—complete with the enthusiastic endorsement of the Royal Family.

In the same year, 1969, the United States recognized the merit of horseback riding not only for its value as a form of recreation and motivation for education, but also for its therapeutic benefits, and the North American Riding for the Handicapped Association (NARHA) was established. A nonprofit organization, NARHA serves as an advisory body to other riding-for-the-disabled groups in America as well as in other countries. It also provides important training, safety guidelines, certification, and low-cost insurance, accrediting therapeutic riding centers to a high standard.

With over 700 equine therapy centers involving an extensive network of 30,000 devoted volunteers, the efficacy of therapeutic riding continues to grow. In America alone, more than 36,000 individuals with cognitive, psychological, or physical disabilities are treated by equine therapists.

Horses have been the instrument of miracles in the lives of thousands of individuals, ranging in age from two to seventy. Those afflicted with such disabilities as cerebral palsy, Down syndrome, autism, multiple sclerosis, and spinal injuries claim substantial improvement in their quality of life, with many experiencing a dramatic healing.

Other than the utter beauty and grace of the animal, what is it that makes the horse such a unique and effective healer for the disabled or handicapped? Throughout history we have depended on horses for our advancement as a civilization. There is no doubt that we have become inexorably linked. Many of us acknowledge the mental/spiritual link that exists between humans and horses, but now, with the help of scientific research, we can understand another element of the power of a horse's healing ability. Results of recent studies, including one done at the University of Delaware, reveal that an actual physical chemistry or connection may exist.

Experiments using reflective dots placed on human participants' back and on the horses' pelvis disclose that the movement of the human body is almost identical to the gait of a horse. A person who is unable to walk, therefore, receives similar motion through the movement of the horse's pelvis when riding a horse. It is the only time many of the patients have ever experienced that "walking input" in their own body. As if by magic, the horse provides the exercise and body movement where it has previously been denied by the human body due to its own disability. The motion stimulates muscles and ligaments that have not been used, and the exercise may eventually enable them to develop to the point of use on their own.

The rocking motion of the horse also encourages balance. Every step the horse takes requires the rider to balance in a countermeasure in order to stay on. Varied positions on the horse work different sets of muscles, as do changing the direction and speed, stopping and starting, working both the horse and the patient. Muscle tone, posture, coordination, and motor development are all improved—in addition to increased self-esteem, confidence, and freedom.

In some cases, the effectiveness of horse therapy may be all about perspective and the ability to see things from a higher point of view.

You may have heard the old story about twin brothers who were given a special gift on their tenth birthday. Presented with a key that would unlock the door of a room, the first boy takes the key, opens the door, and is shocked to see a room full of manure. Horrified and dismayed at such a sight, he turns and runs from the room as fast as his little legs will carry him. The twin brother grabs the key and takes his turn at unlocking the door. As he gazes into the same room full of manure, he jumps for joy and yells out at the top of his lungs: "Wow, with all this manure . . . there has got to be a pony here somewhere!"

A handicapped person is literally given a new perspective on life when sitting or riding on the back of a horse. For the first time, they are lifted to a new "high" from the confines and limitations of their disability. Never before have most of them been able to see life from a height other than the lower vantage point of a wheelchair or a bed. Through the spirit of the horse, as if riding the wind, they can experience a freedom of movement and a joy of feeling larger than life, much bigger than their problems. Their vista has been altered forever.

or a few hours, I thought I'd made the worst mistake of my life in bringing my grandson to his first horse therapy experience," Maurine Gallagher told us. In her weekly prayer group meeting at church, Maurine shared the anguish of heart that she felt over her grandson. Nothing the family tried seemed to come to much. One of her friends in the prayer group told of the dramatic difference that hippotherapy was making in the life of an old school chum she had recently visited during a high school reunion, whose daughter was crippled with multiple sclerosis. Because of the success of a horse therapy program, the eight-year-old girl had eventually gone from barely being able to move (although she had done her best to walk on crutches—painstakingly dragging her legs and feet) to walking freely on her own. Maurine looked into the details and made arrangements to enroll seven-year-old Jamie into a similar local program.

Jamie's tormented little body was bound up and twisted by cerebral palsy, and although therapists assured her that there were many children of various ages in even worse condition in the program, she couldn't imagine how Jamie would even be able to sit on the horse for one second.

"Maybe it was my own fear," Maurine admitted, "but when four people systematically lifted Jamie from his wheelchair and raised him to a specially designed saddle on the horse, I experienced panic at Jamie's flailing movements, as though he was scared to death."

Certified instructors supervised four trained volunteers, all in smooth, caring choreographed movements, and soon Jamie was anchored on a chestnut horse named Robin. Robin remained perfectly calm and still, in spite of the spastic movements and groans of uncertainty made by the little boy, who was now perched precariously high on his back. Other staff members convinced Jamie's grandmother, mother, and father that he would be fine and not to worry.

"For a split second, I thought the horse was going to bolt, and I was stricken with guilt for even bringing Jamie in the first place," Maurine continued. "Then with several gentle strides of Robin's escorted gait, I saw the biggest smile on Jamie's face, the like of which I had never, ever seen before!

"I don't know how to explain it," she continued, "but there is no question that this is a miracle in Jamie's life."

Maurine and the entire family witnessed an unparalleled spark of life enter Jamie with a flame kindled by Robin's spirit. "With the mere mention of the word 'horse,'" she said, "Jamie lights up. He seems to live for the freedom Robin provides for him—like a Pegasus—mounting the air on wings. We have been taking Jamie for horse therapy ever since."

Jamie's family has turned his room into "all things horse." Horse collages, horse blankets, horse pictures, and framed photos of Jamie and Robin surround him with constant reminders of this most special of relationships.

"Whether or not science or psychology can explain the magical connection that occurred between Jamie and the horse, it doesn't matter to us," Maurine said. "We want to do whatever we can to let others know about hippotherapy. It truly has been the miracle that has raised a crippled little boy's body and spirit high above the confinement of seemingly unfair limitations and has given him hope to carry on."

Maurine concludes that she thanks God every day for giving her the key that opened the door to this special equine therapy and for all the wonderful people who made it possible to unleash joy in Jamie's heart.

*M*ost horses used in therapeutic riding are selected because of their reliable and calm temperament, and they undergo extensive training before they are ready to serve as therapists for the disabled. There is no special breed of horse that champions itself over another as ideal therapists, for they include Arabian to Tennessee Walkers and everything in between.

Generally, a special "care plan" is designed for each individual student, as those arriving for therapy vary immensely in degrees of disability. Allowed to progress at their own pace, some students can be so uncertain and frightened that their first session might simply consist of "petting" the horse or sitting on it for a minute.

Basic instruction, including horsemanship, grooming, tacking, and riding skills, is provided in sessions, and if they are able, the students are expected to take care of their horses. Classes include games, exercises, stretches, among other things—on or with the horse— specifically matched with the movement patterns, disposition, and so forth of the student or "patient."

Calvin was diagnosed with spina bifida at birth. His devastated parents were told their beloved infant would never be able to walk, but they refused to accept the finality of the pronouncement. Enrolling Calvin in a special riding program for the handicapped at the age of two years old proved to be a cure beyond their wildest dreams. As Calvin's bond with his special horse therapist—a horse that had been deemed too old to be of much use—grew, his parents were able to observe steady improvement. Five years later, through persistent and regular hippotherapy, Calvin now walks unassisted on his own legs.

Executive director Bethany A. Lee, MS, OTR of the superb Hippotherapy Program of the National Center for Equine Facilitated Therapy (NCEFT) tells of the program's many success stories of lives transformed. Estevan was one such miracle survivor. Premature, he weighed a mere one and one-half pounds at birth, was only twelve inches long, and also suffered from cerebral palsy. By the age of five, Estevan had been through a series of medical procedures but was still totally confined to a wheelchair. Estevan's parents enrolled him in NCEFT hippotherapy, and within one year, they witnessed remarkable improvement in him.

The once-teeny one-and-one-half pounder had gained in strength, confidence, and achievement as he responded to his horse. He progressed to pole vaulting in NCEFT's Therapeutic Vaulting Program! Estevan's parents say the hippotherapy program provided him with a supportive and safe environment that brought a miracle into their lives. In school now, Estevan no longer uses his wheelchair. He walks—even runs to his favorite therapy horse, named Harley!

The first intelligible words spoken by five-year-old Emily, severely autistic from birth, were, "I wuv you horsie!"

It was music to her parents' ears as they followed advice from a special education teacher and counselor to enroll Emily in a hippotherapy program. The first lesson was difficult, as Emily flailed in fear, but when taken off the horse, she suddenly grabbed the horse's leg and hugged it tightly.

"Thank heavens the expert staff and Shadow—the most amazingly calm horse I've ever seen—knew how to handle her," Emily's mother told us.

"After the second lesson, those magic first words Emily uttered out loud, as she once again reached out and hugged Shadow, were the most beautiful words I've ever heard," Emily's mother continued. "How ironic that a horse named Shadow shone a light in Emily's life that sent all the darkness away. What a blessing the horse trainers, therapists, volunteers have given us."

The rescue workers at St. Bernard's Animal Sanctuary in Chesterfield, U.K., had never seen such a miserable pony as Danniboy. The poor old creature had spent all his life tied to a cart, and it was painfully apparent to the staff at St. Bernard's that the pony had never been at all well fed or cared for. His legs were so stiff from being forced to stand in front of a cart all day that he could barely walk. Incredibly, his teeth were overgrown so Danniboy couldn't even eat properly. All in all, he looked mighty scruffy.

Jenny Mark, the manager of St. Bernard's, said that they put him in the field with the forty or so other forsaken horses and ponies, but the miserable Danniboy shunned the company of the others. Although some of the ponies approached the newcomer in a friendly manner, Danniboy wasn't at all interested in acquiring any equine buddies. He preferred to stand alone and apart by himself. In time, the rescue workers managed to nurse him back to physical health, but they were simply unable to move him out of the fog of a dark depression.

Jenny admitted that she and the others at St. Bernard's didn't know what more they could do to cheer up poor Danniboy. At least he was no longer being mistreated, and they saw to it that he was well fed.

Then one day, Sparky, a bedraggled, abandoned tomcat with an injured paw, arrived at the animal sanctuary. Jenny Mark offered him the comforts of her own home, but some inner directive force steered Sparky to Danniboy's stable. Clearly, this was where he wanted to bed down.

At first the gloomy pony took little notice of his uninvited guest, but eventually Sparky's charm won him over. Within a short time, the two became inseparable, and the rescue workers became accustomed to seeing Danniboy grazing in the field with Sparky riding on his back. And when Sparky grew weary of the equestrian posture, he would simply curl up and take a nap atop his friend's ample rear quarters.

The rescue workers at St. Bernard's soon noticed that the bond between horse and cat had made

Danniboy a changed horse. The affection that he felt for Sparky had transformed his depression into contentment.

No animal is ever put down unnecessarily at St. Bernard's, so Danniboy and Sparky will be allowed to live out their natural lives in the fields and stables of the sanctuary.

*H*orse owner Lisa M. Whalen told writer Kimberley Freeman that a horse named Honey has shown her the incredible bond that can take place between humans and horses.

"From the day Honey saved my life—defending me from an enraged, charging horse—to becoming the very protective 'mom' she is now, I've always loved and trusted Honey as my old and faithful friend," Lisa said. "Now that I'm pregnant, Honey likes to place her soft, velvety muzzle on my belly, as if to say 'hi' to the baby growing inside me. She's so very gentle and careful—just as she is with the special needs children who visit her."

Honey, a beautiful red dun chestnut mare, was Lisa Whalen's first horse. Before she bought her, Honey had had little attention and wanted nothing to do with humans.

"Occasionally, someone would tack her up, ride her hard, and throw her back into the paddock, covered in sweat," Lisa told Kimberley. "It took me two months to settle her into a simple walk."

Lisa has owned Honey only since May 4, 2001, but she says that she feels they have already spent a lifetime together. "I'm learning more and more about her every day," she said. "I never could have imagined the wonderful bond that I could have with my horse. She has provided great mental therapy not only for me, but also for the impaired children who come to see her. Every life that Honey has touched has been enlightened in some way."

Sometimes people who knew Honey before Lisa bought her will comment that Honey is a completely different horse. They say even the vet was afraid to go into a stall with Honey, because she'd turn on anyone and kick and bite like she was crazy.

"I didn't know any of this until after I purchased her," Lisa said. "Honey was the first and only horse I looked at, and she walked right up to greet me, like she already knew how it would turn out. My life hasn't been the same since."

Two weeks after Lisa bought Honey, the horse became ill. "I was brand new to the horse world, but I jumped right into learning how to take her temperature, check her vitals, give her medicine, and comfort her,"

Lisa said. "I spent most of my time in her stall until she was better—which turned out to be a real bonding experience. At last, she realized that I was there for her—that I cared and would take care of her no matter what."

Soon after, Honey proved her gratitude and affection when she saved Lisa's life from a crazed horse in a field—one who was charging toward her at top speed.

"It happened one day when a friend and I went into the field to remove Honey's halter and give her an apple," Lisa said. "There was another horse out in the field with Honey who had come from a horrible abuse situation. This horse was big, mean, and dangerous. But I had a friend with me, who said she'd distract the other horse if it looked like there might be any trouble.

"Sure enough, the big, angry horse spotted me," Lisa continued. "He completely ignored my friend, so all I could do was hide behind Honey."

The angry, troubled horse was not fooled by such a maneuver, and he came around Honey, heading straight for Lisa with his ears back, eyes red, and teeth clacking.

Lisa knew that she had to make a run for it. She took a deep breath and took off, but she turned when she heard Honey's squeal.

"There was my little Honey in a fury, charging that big mean horse to drive him away from me,"

Lisa said. "My friend described the look in Honey's eye as, 'Don't you *dare* touch my Lisa!'"

From that moment on, Lisa knew that Honey cared about her as much as she did her, and never again was Lisa afraid to do anything for—or with—her. Honey and she had truly bonded—and nothing was going to stop them now.

The first time Lisa ever cantered, it was on Honey. "Unfortunately, it was also my first fall," Lisa admitted.

Honey stopped immediately and waited calmly for her to get back up. "I wasn't hurt," Lisa said, "so I climbed back on her, and off we went."

Before long, they were riding down roads, across highways, past loud, large vehicles, and into a state park where they spent hours on trails, learning to jump logs, and sometimes galloping bareback down the beach.

"Many times on those park trails," Lisa admitted, "I got us lost. I would just drop the reins and say, 'Honey, take us home.' And she did, every time. We trusted each other, and I knew she would never do anything to hurt me."

One day Lisa removed Honey's saddle after a long trail ride and found a huge welt from a bee sting under the saddle pad. As she examined the swelling, Lisa realized that Honey could have bucked her off when it happened—which would have been any horse's natural instinct—but she held it together. Suddenly, Lisa understood why Honey had continually twitched and shivered during their ride.

"Once a friend got us lost when it was getting dark, and we were stuck in a valley, caught up in thorny vines that tangled around our horse's legs," Lisa recalled. "I slid down and guided Honey out of the thicket, her poor legs bleeding from the cuts. Again, it would have been a natural response for her to buck, but she only shivered, and was careful to keep me safe. Thanks to Honey, we finally found our way out and made it home safely."

Lisa couldn't afford formal riding lessons, so Honey and she became a self-taught team. Lisa already knew that Honey liked trail riding, but she soon learned how much the little mare loved to jump. When a friend offered to trailer them to their first horse show, Lisa and Honey took third place in equitation (the art of horseback riding), fourth place in western pleasure, and fourth in trail class. Lisa was amazed. She had no idea they would be coming home with ribbons that day. Everything they had done, they had learned together.

Lisa told Kimberley Freeman that the next event she and Honey tried was pole bending. "At our very first race," Lisa said, "Honey watched the other horses and riders intently—and when it was our turn, she flew in there as if she'd done this a hundred times before. She shot up the center, wove in and out of the poles, then gave it her all in a pounding gallop back to the gate. She had a ball—and we took first place!"

In the summer of 2003, Lisa and Honey experienced their best trail ride ever and another incredible bonding experience. Lisa decided to ride Honey bareback, attaching a set of reins to her halter, but with no bit and no bridle. Lisa put on her helmet and strapped on a backpack, and they headed off on a two-hour ride through some woods by a beautiful lake.

"When we got to the lake," Lisa said, "I took off my helmet and backpack, and we went right into deep water over our heads. I swam with Honey, beside her and on her back. We bobbed in the waves as the boats came by, waving at us. Honey splashed in the water, and we had a blast. When we were finished swimming, I brought her out to graze on nearby grass while I pulled lunch out of my backpack. I gave her an apple and some cookies. After we both dried off in the sun, I hopped on her back and we headed for home."

Unfortunately, Honey was born of an "accidental" breeding, and therefore Lisa can never register her. "But in my heart," Lisa said, "she's a champion of champions, and I wouldn't trade a moment with my Honey for all the world."

*S*ince about 1984, the Thoroughbred Retirement Foundation, the largest and oldest thoroughbred rescue operation in the United States, has operated work programs in partnership with such penal institutions as the Blackburn Correctional Facility in Lexington, Kentucky; the Marion County Correctional Institution in Lowell, Florida; and the Wallkill Correctional Facility in Wallkill, New York. In these unique programs, retired or discarded thoroughbred horses that were former track favorites and champions, as well as losers and also-rans, are allowed to live out their lives being well cared for by prison inmates. Jim Tremper, the program's director at the Wallkill facility, explained to Mike Wise of *The New York Times* (August 10, 2003) that they've rescued horses that had been cruelly discarded, some even left for dead in their stables.

Tremper said that he had seen the thoroughbreds change the prisoners' lives as much as the prisoners had changed the horses'. Many of the more violent inmates had a history of intimidating other people with their size and strength. When they came up against the bulk and power of the thoroughbreds, many of them found themselves humbled for the first time in their lives.

The inmates who tend the horses must earn the right by exhibiting good behavior for two years. In addition, they must have three years or less remaining before their earliest release to be assigned to the program. Wallkill Correctional Facility is their last or next-to-last place of confinement before parole.

Horse racing buffs would be amazed to learn the number of former top purse winners that have been rescued by the Foundation. There's Quick Call, a former Saratoga favorite, winner of sixteen races and $807,817 in earnings; Klabin's Gold, winner of the 1998 Hirsch Jacobs Stakes at Pimlico; and Banker's Jet, who earned close to a million dollars in his career. These great champions were found starved, underweight, abused, some with fractured legs, and nearly all existing in deplorable conditions before finding a home in pastures next to guard towers and being groomed by inmates rather than trainers.

And while these noble steeds suffered before the Thoroughbred Retirement Foundation reclaimed their lives, their fate was far superior to a number of Kentucky Derby winners, Breeders' Cup Classic favorites, and Jockey Club Gold winners that have been slaughtered for pet food. According to the Foundation, the number of horses of all breeds butchered in the United States for sale as meat abroad or as pet food domestically has been declining steadily—from nearly 350,000 in the 1980s to about 60,000 in 2001. Approximately 30,000 thoroughbreds are born each year in the United States, and the Foundation estimates that as many as 3,000 to 5,000 are retired annually. Only the well-known and high-profile champions will receive comfortable retirements or become studs on prominent breeding farms.

The Foundation was founded by Monique Koehler, who owned an advertising agency in New York. Seed money was raised from a fundraiser at Belmont Park in 1983, and from the breeders and owners of Secretariat, Kelso, and Forego, whom Ms. Koehler persuaded to help less-fortunate retired thoroughbreds. When she sought green pastures for the rescued horses, Ms. Koehler learned that many prison systems owned thousands of unused acres. A number of correctional facilities agreed that the partnership between inmates and rescued racehorses was an ideal match of individuals looking for a second chance and an opportunity for rehabilitation.

*M*illie Unger, who declares herself "eighty-three years young," still lives in her own apartment near the New Jersey neighborhood in which she was born and reared. Although Millie considers herself thoroughly modern, one memory of yesteryear that she regrets contemporary kids will never experience is that of seeing and hearing the milkman with his wagon and horse as they made the rounds from house to house.

"When my own children were small, I used to tell them how the bottles would *clink-clink* together and the wagon would squeak and the horse's hooves would go *clop-clop* and make much more delightful music than the ice cream trucks and their blaring tunes today," Millie said. "My kids, Ethel and Irvin, used to like to hear about one of my misadventures with our milkman, Clarence, and his big old horse, Bucephalus."

It would be many years before Millie would know the whimsy that Clarence had employed when he named his milk-wagon horse Bucephalus. "I found out when I studied world history in tenth grade that Bucephalus was the name of Alexander the Great's horse," she said. "When the incident occurred, I was only about three, and I called him 'Boosey.'"

Clarence and Bucephalus would arrive in their neighborhood around 8:00 in the morning, and when the weather was pleasant, little Millie, along with her five-year-old sister, Agnes, and the five-and-a-half-year-old neighbor boy, Danny, would run to meet them.

"We would hear Boosey's big hooves going *clop-clop, clop-clop* on the hard pavement, and if it wasn't raining or freezing cold, we would be there to welcome them to our neighborhood," Millie said. "Our street was last on Clarence's route, and when he had finished delivering his morning round of milk, he let Boosey have a drink of cool water from the fountain on Martin Street. In 1923, there were not many drinking fountains for horses left in the city. A lot of them had been torn down when people began to use more automobiles than horses. But a few fountains had been left standing, and the big fountain on Martin Street was one of them. It was kind of oval-shaped, like a huge bathtub, and there was a smaller drinking fountain for dogs at the foot."

Millie recalled how Agnes, Danny, and she would run along toward the fountain beside Bucephalus. Danny had a little ritual in which he would call out to the milkman that he would race them to the fountain. The good-natured Clarence would accept the challenge and gently slap Bucephalus's reins.

"Get up, there, you noble steed," Clarence would urge the horse in mock earnestness. "We're racing Danny Boy."

The old white horse wouldn't quicken his pace one bit. He kept on going down the street with a steady *clop-clop, clop-clop,* just the way he always did.

"Danny would reach the fountain first and ecstatically cry out that he had won," Millie said. "Agnes would get there a little ahead of me, and Boosey and I would reach the fountain about the same time. Old Boosey didn't care who won. What he wanted was a drink of cool water. He would thrust his muzzle down deep and gulp in big mouthfuls."

The next part of the children's morning ritual came when the milkman would ask the children to watch Bucephalus for a minute while he went into Morgenstern's Diner and got a cup of coffee. Clarence knew that the horse would never start moving unless he was in the wagon, but he always told the children to watch him just the same.

"When Boosey had had enough to drink, he began playing," Millie said. "He would hold his muzzle under the water and blow air through his nostrils, making a funny gurgling noise. Then he would raise his head with a jerk as if he were trying to splash water on us."

Danny tried his best to sound like Clarence and tell Bucephalus, "Whoa there, old boy. Steady, boy." Then he patted the old horse gently.

Millie said that in those days there was a small park next to the drinking fountain, and the children would gather some fresh green grass and giggle when Boosey would nibble the treat from their open hands.

"On this particular day, Danny and Agnes had brought Boosey a couple of apples that they had saved from their lunches the afternoon before, and they were so busy feeding the big horse the extra-special treat that they didn't notice that I had climbed onto the edge of the dogs' drinking fountain and had tried to pull myself up to the big horse trough above it," Millie said. "I wanted to get closer to Boosey so that I could feed him the grass that I had picked for him and pat his muzzle and say, 'Steady, boy' the way Danny did. I hooked my arms over the edge of the trough and squirmed and wriggled. Then all of a sudden, I fell into the water."

Millie recalled that the cold water was quite deep, at least for a three-year-old, and she sputtered and gasped as she kept slipping and sliding.

"I could hear both Danny and Agnes screaming for Clarence to come to help them get me out of the fountain," Millie said. "I suppose unless someone pulled me out of there pretty fast, I might even have drowned."

But before either Clarence, Agnes, or Danny could reach her, Millie felt something grab the back of her dress and lift her out of the water.

"I will never forget that sensation of being jerked from the cold water and lifted high into the air," Millie said. "Good old Boosey had come to the rescue and had grabbed my little pink dress with his teeth and yanked me out of the trough."

As he set Millie gently on the ground at the base of the fountain, her dress tore and Bucephalus was left with a patch of pink cloth stuck in his teeth.

"I had started to cry with fear and panic," Millie said, "but when I saw Boosey standing there with a piece of my dress in his mouth while water dripped and dribbled all around, I began to laugh. Pretty soon everyone was laughing at the soaked little girl and cheering the big old milk horse that had rescued her. Mrs. Morgenstern came out to ask if I was okay, and I told her I was just fine. Boosey had saved me."

When Clarence took Millie in his arms to lift her up so she could give Boosey a big hug for being her hero, he chuckled and said that from now on instead of asking the kids to watch Bucephalus, he was going to tell Bucephalus to watch them.

*F*or many horse racing enthusiasts around the world, the name Man o' War is synonymous with the ideal champion that always crosses the finish line several lengths ahead of the pack. Today, over eighty years since Man o' War last set hoof on a track, he remains a household name. Only time will tell if the memory of his fame will one day be surpassed by that of one of his grandsons, Seabiscuit.

Man o' War was foaled by the mare Muhubah on March 29, 1917. The colt had been sired by Fair Play, one of the sons of Hastings, a racing legend of the previous century. Although an early trainer thought that the colt had a special fire in the eyes, as a yearling Man o' War was a very unimpressive horse, with legs so long and skinny that he still looked like a young foal.

In 1918, his owner, August Belmont II, brought Man o' War to the Saratoga Yearling sale and sold him to Samuel Riddle. Riddle was encouraged to make the purchase by Louis Feustel, a horse trainer who had worked with both Hastings and Fair Play. As a ten-year-old boy, Feustel had been thrilled when he was allowed to gallop the fiery Hastings, and he predicted that the gangly yearling possessed the same grit as his grandfather.

Within a few months, the skinny colt had filled out into a magnificent horse with a healthy chestnut coat and an imposing presence. He was nicknamed "Big Red" by his trainers, and they all knew that this horse could not be held back once he hit the tracks.

In Man o' War's debut at Belmont Park on June 6, 1919, he had no difficulty winning by six lengths. Given a three-day rest, Man o' War ran in his first stakes race at Keene Memorial and effortlessly won again. Eleven days later, he triumphed at the Youthful Stakes at Jamaica Park, and with only a two-day breather, he won the Hudson Stakes at Aqueduct by several lengths. Man o' War had another rest, of twelve days, then snatched the Tremont Stakes from his challengers before he went upstate to Saratoga where he defeated his chief threat, Upset, to win the United States Hotel Stakes by a length.

On August 13, 1919, Man o' War suffered his only defeat in a race that still raises the blood pressure of racing historians. As controversial and as unfair as the event may seem even to those separated from the ill-fated race by almost ninety years, the loss did little to damage Big Red's reputation as one of the greatest racehorses that ever galloped on a track.

The race in question was the Sanford Memorial at Saratoga. Once again the horse Upset was entered in the event, but he was considered of little consequence since Man o' War defeated him in the Tremont Stakes eleven days earlier. Racing experts predicted that the only horse that would give Big Red a run for his money in the six-furlong race would be Golden Broom. Man o' War had now filled out to 970 pounds, not large for a thoroughbred, but those once-skinny legs were now pulsing with power.

In the early 1900s, there was no starting gate to launch the horses into a spirited race. Rather, the jockeys would circle their mounts, then approach the starting line and await the signal of the starter's flag that the race had begun. As fate would have it, Man o' War was still circling and was facing away from the starting line when the starter dropped the flag and signaled the beginning of the race. Before his jockey had Big Red turned around, the other horses were thundering down the track.

As if Man o' War took the unfair start personally, he ran as he had never run before. Within very little time, Big Red was passing his competitors, but the other riders were pleased to press their advantage and saw to it that their mounts kept the favorite from taking the rail, the shortest route to the finish line. Incredibly, in spite of his delayed start and his being boxed in by the other horses, Man o' War lost to the well-named Upset by only half a length.

Although Big Red had lost the race, he had won the hearts of the racing world. He was praised for his remarkable feat of overcoming the unfair start, and the majority of racing buffs declared that there was no question that Big Red was the best horse in the race. Man o' War had lost the Sanford Memorial, but he received all the glory, as if he had won.

Ten days later, at the Grand Union Hotel Stakes, Man o' War handily defeated Upset, reasserting his position as Number One. Big Red was to face Upset three more times in their racing careers. He easily defeated Upset in all three races, but Upset would still go down in racing history as the only horse to defeat Man o' War.

Big Red never raced in the Kentucky Derby, because his owner, Sam Riddle, just didn't like to race in that state. Riddle had no objections to Man o' War's entering the Preakness, ten days after the Derby.

The horse Paul Jones, winner of the 1920 Derby, and several other Derby contenders were eager to face Man o' War and see if he had what it took to run against horses of their caliber. Big Red won by 1½ lengths. His nemesis Upset was second.

In his next race, the Withers, Man o' War defeated Wildair by two lengths and set a new American record for the mile in 1:35 4/5. Next, at the Belmont Stakes, he set another American record of 1⅜ miles in 2:14 1/5. At the Stuyvesant Handicap, Big Red won by eight lengths at the finish line.

At the Dwyer Stakes at Aqueduct, Big Red met another powerful contender for the second time. John P. Grier was a horse that many racing historians believe had the greatest potential to challenge the champion, and the experts of the day generally agreed that he was the second best colt of his generation. Man o' War set another record of 1:49 1/5 in the Dwyer Stakes, but John P. Grier was only 1½ lengths behind him at the finish line.

Big Red dusted off both Upset and John P. Grier in the Travers Stakes, and by the time he returned to Belmont for the Lawrence Realization, there weren't too many horse owners eager to pit their contenders against the mighty charger, who now weighed in at 1,150 pounds. At Belmont, Louis Feustel, Big Red's longtime trainer, felt the only challenge to the three-year-old champion would be the clock. The record for the 1⅝-mile track was 2:45. Feustel told the jockey to shatter it. Man o' War beat the old records by nearly five seconds, and he won the race by an estimated 100 lengths.

One week later, Big Red set yet another American record at the Jockey Club Stakes: 2:28 4/5 for 1½ miles.

But even the mightiest of champions finally faces the effects of stress, physical exertion, and a constant striving for excellence. Shortly after the Jockey Club Stakes, Big Red bowed a tendon in the process of defeating a large field of challengers at the Potomac Handicap, which included Wildair, Blazes, and Paul Jones.

Feustel and the trainers worked carefully with Man o' War, giving his sore leg special attention. They managed to keep Big Red fit enough to win the Kenilworth Park Gold Cup, defeating the principal challenger, Sir Barton, by seven lengths.

Although Man o' War had won the race in spite of his injured leg, a great deal of ill will and accusations clouded the event. Some said that Sir Barton's sore feet were the only reason he lost. Other owners were bitter that their horses were not invited to participate against Man o' War. And to add to the dark atmosphere, Feustel discovered that Big Red's stirrup had been cut by someone before the race. Fortunately the leather strap had managed to hold together without dumping the jockey on the track. All things considered, it seemed time to retire Big Red.

On January 28, 1921, Man o' War was ridden under silks at the Lexington Association and received a rousing response from a huge crowd. Although Sam Riddle had not allowed Big Red to race in Kentucky, the horse did set foot on a Kentucky racetrack to make his final public appearance. Although many offers for match races were presented to Riddle and purses of large sums were offered, all races were declined.

Man o' War died on November 1, 1947, at the age of thirty. His remains lie under a heroic bronze statue of his likeness at the Kentucky Horse Park in Lexington.

*V*ernon Blankenship told us of the challenge he faced during the summer when he was seventeen and working for his uncle Galen Moss. "Uncle Galen said that part of my chores on the farm was to make a horse named Olga happy," he said. "Since I lived in the city and had never been around horses before, I had no idea what would make a seemingly ornery, unfriendly mare happy."

Galen was Vernon's mom's oldest brother. "He worked the Moss family farm outside a small town in southern Wisconsin," Vernon said. "Uncle Galen was a tall, thin man with a kind of grumpy manner. He wore faded bib overalls, a battered straw hat, and he always had several days' growth of whiskers that he always shaved before he could sprout a respectable beard. Galen had never married, and Mom always said it was no wonder, because when he was a kid he was already stubborn as a mule and set in his ways.

"In the fall of 1988, I was going to be a senior in high school," Vernon explained, "and I was in need of a summer job to help with my nest egg for college. Although I was a 'big city boy' from a suburb of Milwaukee, Galen said that I could work for him. Since we had often visited the farm at various times of the year, I was not totally ignorant of farmwork."

When Vernon arrived on the farm in June, he discovered that his uncle had purchased a horse. Vernon was puzzled by this new acquisition to the livestock because he knew that there hadn't been a horse on the Moss farm in years. Uncle Galen explained that he bought the horse, a Norwegian Fjord, because he thought his little nieces and nephews would love to ride a horse when they came to the farm. Surely, he said, the addition of a horse to the farm would encourage his three sisters, who had all married and moved away, to visit more often with their children.

Vernon agreed that might be true. He was the oldest of nine cousins, and he would have very much enjoyed horseback riding around the barnyard and the pasture when he was younger. He knew that his sisters—nine-year-old Karen and thirteen-year-old Beth—would love to ride a horse when they came to visit Uncle Galen. The immediate problem, as Vernon saw it, was the fact that Olga seemed kind of standoffish and aloof.

"Have you ridden her, Uncle Galen?" Vernon asked, as he walked closer to the pen in which Olga stood chewing a mouthful of hay, seeming to study his every movement. The mare was cream colored, with a dark dorsal stripe. She was not very tall, but she had a thick neck and shoulders and a broad chest.

"She's supposed to be a good horse," Galen said, avoiding the direct question. "Old Mr. Swenson, who sold her to me, said that his great-grandfather brought the original stock from western Norway. According to him, the breed is one of the oldest and best in Europe. Swenson said she'd be a good horse as long as she was happy."

"How do you keep a horse happy?" Vernon wondered.

Uncle Galen scratched his head and shrugged. "I haven't got the faintest idea. I've never owned a horse before. To tell you the truth, when I was a little boy and your grandpa kept a couple of horses that he liked to ride, I always thought they weren't too intelligent. Matter of fact, I never really liked horseback riding. When grandpa would take me along on Sunday afternoon trail rides with his riding club, I was always pretty much bored and wishing I was

somewhere else, doing something else. I just bought
Olga because I wanted a horse around for the kids
when they visited."

Vernon winced at the realization that his uncle
had purchased the horse simply as an entertainment
for his nieces and nephews, but he himself really had
little interest in the animal. Vernon didn't know
much about horses, but he felt that any animal could
sense if it were wanted or not.

"Uncle Galen," Vernon resubmitted the question
that his uncle had avoided answering, "have you ridden the horse?"

"I saddled her up a couple of times, but I didn't
really ride her," he admitted. "I thought I would add
riding Olga to your list of chores. You find a way to
make Olga happy, and I guess she'll let you ride her.
Once you've ridden her, she'll be willing to let your
sisters and all your little cousins sit in her saddle."

Vernon stood quietly for a few moments, considering
the situation. He had this strange feeling that Olga was
somehow sending him a silent plea that he approach her
with gentleness and treat her with kindness. He learned
that Uncle Galen had owned her for about three weeks,
and all that time she had been largely neglected, sen-
tenced to the prison of a small pen and her stall.

"I'll give you the pickup to drive into town any
night you want and go to the picture shows," Uncle

Galen said, sharpening the bargain. "And I'll even buy all the gas."

"It's a deal," said Vernon, and he shook hands with Uncle Galen to seal the bargain.

But that very first night Vernon found out that making Olga happy was no easy job. Maybe she did have a problem of some sort that wouldn't be easy to remove.

Olga made such a noise and a fuss when Uncle Galen brought the cows in the barn to be milked that Vernon was taken by surprise. Olga stamped her front hooves and tugged at the rope that kept her in her stall.

"She always makes a commotion when the cows come in," Uncle Galen shouted over the din. "I swear that horse is crazy."

Vernon decided to bring Olga over to the other end of the barn, away from all the cows. He filled her stall with clean hay, and he gave her plenty of cracked corn and oats to eat.

But Olga still didn't act happy. She just looked at Vernon, stretched out her neck, flopped her ears, and made a long, sad noise, as if she were blowing her nose.

"I stayed with her a long time that night," Vernon said. "I talked to her, and I tried to pet her, but she withdrew and stamped her left front hoof, as if warning me to back off. So I respected her wishes, and just stood outside her stall, talking softly to her."

The next morning Uncle Galen led Olga from her stall to the small pasture next to the corncrib. Over his left shoulder he carried tack that had been hanging in a corner of the barn. He placed the bridle on Olga and showed Vernon how to saddle a horse. Olga stood patiently, seemingly detached from the process, as Galen tightened the cinch around her middle.

"I had only been on a horse a few times in my life," Vernon recalled. "Uncle Galen told me to put my foot in the stirrup and sit in the saddle like I knew what I was doing. Horses, he added, had to know who was the boss."

Vernon admitted that he was really nervous. He had visions of himself flying through the air like some rodeo contestant thrown from a wild mustang. He gritted his teeth when his vision included a vivid picture of him landing very hard upon the ground.

When Vernon said, "Giddap!" and dug his heels into Olga's flanks, she took about three steps forward, and then she stopped. She stopped still, and she stayed still.

"You have to show a horse who's boss!" Uncle Galen said again. "You have to make her understand that you are the kingpin and you are going to ride her where you want to go and she has to obey you! She has no say in the matter!"

But Olga would not budge an inch no matter how many times Uncle Galen and Vernon yelled, "Giddap."

"I guess she's not happy yet," Vernon said. "And I can't convince her that I'm the boss, either."

"I guess not," Uncle Galen grumbled. "It's not your fault. She's just stupid and stubborn."

Then Vernon had an idea. "Maybe she's hungry," he said, and he dashed into the barn for some hay.

He returned and tickled the horse's nose with the sweet-smelling clover hay. Olga just stared at Vernon, then she stretched out her neck, flapped her ears, and let out a big sneeze.

"Put her back in the barn," said Uncle Galen angrily. "There's no use wasting our whole morning with that horse when we have a lot of work to do."

Vernon put Olga back in her stall. "Just as I started to walk away and go about my morning chores," he said, "Olga made a soft kind of whinnying sound. It really touched my heart, because it sounded like she was saying that she was sorry. And, at the same time, she was begging me to understand why she was so sad and miserable."

About an hour later Uncle Galen ran up to Vernon and shouted his alarm and concern. "The new black calf that I showed you last night has disappeared," he said. "Go find it, Vernon. It can't have gone far."

Vernon looked in all the stalls, but he didn't see the black calf. "He's not here," Vernon said, "unless he's with Olga."

"Look in her stall," Uncle Galen said in desperation. "I sure hope that calf hasn't wandered in with Olga. That darn horse would probably kick it to pieces."

Vernon reached the stall first and saw that the calf had strayed into Olga's stall. But Olga wasn't kicking the calf. She was licking it. The two animals were rubbing noses as friendly as could be.

"Move over, Olga!" ordered Uncle Galen, and Olga obediently moved so that Uncle Galen could get in her stall.

"Hey!" said Vernon in surprise. "She minded you."

Uncle Galen scratched his head. "So she did," he said.

"Maybe she's happy now," Vernon said. "Let's try to saddle her up again."

So Uncle Galen led Olga out to the barnyard and the black calf followed.

"Giddap," said Uncle Galen when he had saddled and mounted Olga. And off Olga trotted with the calf frisking beside her.

"Hurray!" Vernon shouted. "I think Olga is happy now."

Suddenly it all seemed so obvious to Vernon. Olga had been used to being penned with cattle and had come to regard them as her family and friends.

"Later, we verified this with Mr. Swenson, who had sold Olga to Uncle Galen," Vernon said. "Daily, Swenson had ridden her out to bring the cattle home in the evenings, and Olga had her stall in the barn next to the herd. She had been so lonely in the stall by herself after Uncle Galen bought her and brought her to his farm. That was why she always fussed so when the cattle came in the barn to be milked. She just wanted to be near them."

"I guess Olga's not so stupid and mean after all," Uncle Galen admitted. "All she wanted was some friends. Anybody's happier with friends."

Vernon concluded his story by saying that Olga was the reigning queen of Uncle Galen's farm for many years, and she was certainly one of the contributing factors in all his little cousins' wanting to visit Uncle Galen as often as possible.

"She was always gentle with the kids, and she loved the sound of their laughter as she trotted around the pastures with them happily on her back," Vernon said. "Whenever I had a long holiday while I was in college, I would visit Uncle Galen and take Olga for a long ride along the creek. Olga never seemed unhappy— and I know she was never lonely again."

The debate over whether or not animals have souls will not likely be resolved to everyone's satisfaction. Those individuals who have formed a firm bond of love with their pet will often say that if Heaven doesn't allow their cat, dog, or horse within its pearly gates, then they aren't going in without them. Although others are uncertain as to animals' having an eternal spirit that will grant them an afterlife, down through the centuries a good many sober, sincere witnesses have reported their encounter with animal ghosts.

Purdue University veterinarian Dina Andrews told writer Marigrace Heyer that in 1991 she was making a house call in a Los Angeles suburb where a white horse had been reported sick by its owners. It was dusk when Dr. Andrews arrived, and she noticed another white horse in the same corral as the horse that was quite obviously ill. She thought nothing of the presence of the other horse, but later as she was going over instructions for the sick horse with the owner, she mentioned that the two horses should be separated until the ailing horse was better.

After she had uttered those words, the owners looked at her like she was crazy and asked her what in the world she was talking about—they didn't have two horses.

Veterinarian Andrews was puzzled by their response, but she patiently described in detail the horse that she had seen in the corral with the sick one.

The astonished owners said that she had given the exact description of an old horse of theirs that had died recently. They could only wonder if the ghost horse had come back to watch over its sick companion.

Justin and Tanya Poole told us of the time that they were camping out in the desert near the Superstition Mountains in Arizona and encountered a ghostly herd of mustangs. "This was shortly after we were married in 1974," Justin said. "The area around Apache Junction and Mesa wasn't nearly as spread out and populated as it is today. If you liked to camp out under the stars in those days, you didn't have to drive too far outside of Phoenix."

According to the Pooles, sometime around 1:00 in the morning, they were awakened by horses stepping around them in their sleeping bags. They were astonished to find themselves literally surrounded by a herd of about twenty mustangs grazing on the sparse vegetation.

"Clearly, in the flickering light of our dying campfire and in the soft, silver light of a full moon, we could see the horses grazing all around us," Justin said.

"Neither of us could be considered horse enthusiasts," Tanya admitted, "but we were thrilled to see the beautiful horses moving around us. We both whispered what a wonderful bonus gift this was to our camping trip." The Pooles knew that the Southwest used to be the home of many herds of wild mustangs. They were also aware that the breed basically traces its origin back to the horses that somehow got away from the early Spanish explorers. In frontier times and even much later, cowboys used to try to capture the tough and sturdy horses and make them into cow horses.

The Pooles were amazed that a herd the size of the one that surrounded them could thrive so near the metropolitan area of Phoenix, Scottsdale, and Mesa. "We were even more amazed that none of the horses seemed to pay either of us the slightest bit of attention," Justin said. "And we were surprised that they would come so near our campfire. For a while, neither of us dared move for fear of scaring them off. We just wanted to observe them for as long as we could."

After about half an hour, Justin wanted to take a picture of the mustangs. As quietly as possible, he crawled out of his sleeping bag and walked slowly toward the van where he had left his camera. He moved cautiously around the grazing horses, careful not to touch or disturb them.

"I got the camera from the van," Justin said. "I knew that the first flash would undoubtedly scare off the entire herd, but Tanya agreed with me that it was worth the chance. We wanted something to prove our beautiful experience with the rare mustang herd."

Justin set the camera for the appropriate shutter speed and turned around slowly to take his best shot. But there were no horses in sight.

"Where did they go?" he demanded of Tanya.

Tanya was sitting up in her sleeping bag, blinking her eyes in bafflement. "I don't know. They just went."

Tanya explained to us that she had witnessed the entire herd suddenly "evaporate." Still marveling over the experience of nearly thirty years ago, Tanya said, "They didn't run away, they didn't walk away, they just disappeared. It was as if we had been watching someone's home movies and the plug got pulled on the projector. The picture of the horses just went dark all at once."

When morning came, Tanya and Justin found no trace of the herd anywhere around their campsite. There was not even a single hoofprint to prove the mustangs had ever been there.

"It was at that point that we had to admit the truth of what we had been denying ever since the herd disappeared," Tanya said. "We had been surrounded by a herd of ghost horses."

Justin concluded the Pooles' story by saying that over the years since their encounter with the ghostly mustangs, they had heard other stories of individuals who had witnessed similar manifestations of ghost horses moving silently through the night, like shadows from a once-glorious past.

Joseph F., who lives on the small family ranch that his great-grandfather established in Oklahoma in 1875, told us that their livestock is watched over by a ghost horse.

"Great-grandfather Ethan was a pretty tough hombre when he came to the territory after the Civil War," Joseph told us. "He had been a factory worker in Pittsburgh, and when he was mustered out of the Union Army in 1865 at age twenty-two, all he had to his name was the government-issue horse that he had ridden as a supply sergeant, a cap-lock Springfield musket, and twenty dollars. He decided he wanted nothing more of factories, and he headed West with two friends."

Ethan worked for eight years for a wealthy rancher, who rewarded the war veteran's untiring and diligent service by giving him a few head of cattle and helping him stake out his own ranch. Ethan had lost one friend to renegades on the trip to the territory, and another had kept on riding to Texas. His best friend through all those years was the old army horse that he had named Star because of the irregular-shaped white patch on the forehead of an otherwise shiny black body. Star had proven to be a fine cow horse and a stalwart companion.

"Great-grandpa lived in a combination tent and sod hut for a couple of years before he managed to build a crude house on the ranch," Joseph said. "His herd was coming along just fine, and he even managed to find time to court Maybelle, the daughter of a nearby rancher, who became my great-grandma."

Then on a bright Sunday afternoon, tragedy struck Ethan's small ranch.

"Great-grandma was a religious person, and she talked Ethan into attending Sunday meetings in town, about six miles away," Joseph explained. "By this time, Ethan had managed to obtain a couple more horses and a buggy. He would never subject his old friend Star to the indignity of being hitched to a buggy, so he put the reins to another horse and left the ranch under the supervision of his trusted companion."

When the couple returned from the religious observance in town, they were horrified to discover Star lying dead outside of his corral. He had been shot many times, and it was plain to Ethan to piece together the details of the terrible scene that had taken place while they were away.

"Rustlers had visited the ranch," Joseph said. "Ethan could establish that they had led away the other horse in the corral and that they tried to steal Star as well as the cattle. Ethan figured from the evidence scattered around the yard that his old friend had put up such a fight protecting the cattle that the rustlers had shot him half a dozen times and skedaddled before they were discovered in their crime."

Ethan mourned Star for the best friend that he had ever had. He dragged the carcass to the top of a hill overlooking the ranch and buried him. Sometimes he would sit for hours at the graveside. The two of them had come from Pennsylvania twelve years before to build a new life. They had worked together long, hard hours many a day and on through the night to build a herd of cattle and establish a ranch. Old Star just wasn't going to let some worthless saddle tramps take all that away. And he died protecting it.

A few weeks later, a little before dark, Ethan was riding herd together with a couple of ranch hands that he had just hired. He happened to look toward the hill where Star lay resting, and he swore that he saw his old friend standing there, big and black against the twilight sky. Star rose up on his back legs and pawed the air with his forelegs—and then he was gone.

Ethan knew that he had seen the ghost of Star, and he sensed that the spirit of the horse had returned to warn him. When Ethan looked away from Star's graveyard, he saw three plumes of dust far off in the distance. Somehow he knew those three riders coming across the plain were the rustlers returning to hit his herd after dark. Forewarned by the ghost of Star, Ethan and his two ranch hands were waiting in ambush for the rustlers. The outlaws surrendered without putting up any resistance, and Ethan and his men trussed them up and brought them to the sheriff in the back of the buggy.

"On another occasion, about four months later," Joseph said, "Ethan once again looked toward Star's grave and saw an image of the ghost horse. In the next few minutes, Ethan saw dark clouds gathering. Immediately he told his ranch hands to bunch the herd. He suddenly knew that Star was warning him that there was a big storm coming, one that would have lots of thunder that would frighten the cattle. Within an hour, the sky was filled with crashing thunder and flashes of lightning. Great-grandpa was convinced that the ghost of Star had come to warn him to prepare the herd and to guard against a stampede."

Since that time, it has become tradition that the ghost of Star will appear to warn the family of danger.

Joseph claims to have seen the spirit horse himself. "It was a beautiful day in early December," he recalled. "My herd isn't that large, but it is important to me. I had let it out of the corrals to graze when I just happened to glance toward the hill that overlooks the ranch and saw a big black horse rearing up on its back legs. I wondered where the horse had come from—and then it disappeared before my eyes. I knew it was old Star come to warn me about something. My grandpa and my dad had both told me that they had seen the ghost horse and had been able to avert a terrible event because of its warning them in time.

"Suddenly, just as clear as if someone had shouted at me, I heard the word 'blizzard.' Although it seemed such a pleasant day, I called to my wife and son to help me drive the cattle back to the corrals and barn. Later that day, we were hit with a heavy snow and high winds. I would have been certain to have lost several head of cattle. There is no question in my mind, Star still watches over our ranch."

*W*riter Kimberley Freeman sent us an interview that she had conducted with horse owner Cheryl Williams regarding the beautiful seven-year-old Palomino Haflinger named Mikey who had been working with them in a riding therapy program for children since he was three years old.

Mikey is a beautiful shade of gold with a thick white mane and tail, and Cheryl said that some of the program's most intimate moments around the barn occurred as the children brushed his luxuriously thick hair. "Whether it be the sharing of confidences, tears of grief for a much-loved parent or grandparent, or sometimes giggles over trying to find just the right hairstyle to impress a cute boy," she commented, "there's just something about 'Mikey's Magic Mane.'"

Mikey will stand for hours as the kids pamper and brush him, and Ms. Williams suggested that his infinite patience may be what contributes to his extraordinary ability to sense what the children are feeling. He seems to know just what each child needs in terms of love and self-esteem.

According to Cheryl Williams: "Recently, we were conducting a session with a boy and his father. The two had been having a problem communicating with one another after a divorce in the family. In an effort to try to get them working together, I asked the boy to teach his father how to ground-tie Mikey.

"First the boy demonstrated, then explained the process of asking Mikey to 'stay.' He insisted that his father whisper in the horse's ear to let him know what to do before dropping the lead rope.

"The father followed his son's instructions— minus the whisper—and sure enough, Mikey walked away. Again, the son stressed the importance of telling Mikey what was expected of him, patiently instructing his father about the importance of good communication. Once the man finally whispered into the horse's ear, Mikey stood completely still and stayed focused on the man as he walked to the other end of the arena."

Later, she asked the father what he had whispered to Mikey, and he told her, "My son said I have to really believe, and that I had to trust Mikey, so I told him just that!"

Later that day, Cheryl Williams received an excited call from the father. "He told me that after our session at the barn, he'd had a revelation," she said. "He'd decided to drop the custody battle with his wife after seeing what 'real communication' could do."

What the father never knew, Cheryl explained later to Kimberley Freeman, was that Mikey knew exactly how to ground tie, and she suspects that he didn't do it that day for a reason. "He was waiting for the two humans to get their communication straight first," she concluded. "Once again, our wise Mikey had been the intermediary in bringing two people together."

*P*enelope Smith, author of *Animal Talk,* said recently that there are now at least 200 animal communicators in the United States. Asia Voight of Stoughton, Wisconsin, told Doug Moe of the Madison *Capital Times* (September 11, 2003) that she has "talked and listened" to about 6,000 animals over the last six years. Ms. Voight compared her telepathic communication with animals to prayer: "It's how we communicate with God. Most people pray and think that God can hear them."

Brad Steiger claims that his sister June became a "horse whisperer" back in the early 1950s, long before either the term or the ability became well known.

Like so many young girls, June was absolutely wild about horses. When they went to the double-feature western movies on Saturday night, Brad might be lost in the fantasy of the Old West, but June would be lost in the fantasy of having a horse of her own and riding effortlessly across the prairie the way the western heroes rode across the silver screen.

Then, in the late summer of 1952, when she was twelve years old, June's dream came true. She accompanied their parents to a livestock sale barn where once a month a horse auction was held. Their father spotted a quarter horse mare in the pens, and he said that if it seemed she could be bought for a fair price, he would buy her for June. June's heartbeat kept tempo with the chant of the auctioneer, and she nearly jumped up and screamed with delight when their father had the winning bid.

June named the mare Lady, and the horse proved to be a gentle, dependable animal, already trained to ride and to be patient with youthful riders. June spent hours with her horse, becoming daily more accomplished in the saddle.

The quarter horse is the classic horse of the American cowboy. The breed is a heavily muscled animal, a descendent of the thoroughbred and a popular family horse. The quarter horse derives its name from its remarkable speed in short distances and sprints, and the cowboys' assertion that there is no horse that can run faster for a "quarter" of a mile.

If Lady had arrived a few years earlier, Brad might have been a bit jealous of his sister's having a horse, but at sixteen, he was more interested in the "horses" under his 1941 Chevrolet. Besides, he had his calves to work with and train to halter for showing in the county fair.

Although their father had bought one horse for a fair price at the sale barn, Lady turned out to yield an unexpected dividend when it gradually became evident that she was pregnant. Since they had no way of knowing when she had been bred, they had no way of estimating when Lady would foal. The gestation period for horses is 333 days, eleven months, give or take a couple of days. All they could do was to wait, let Nature run its course, and be observant.

One morning in April of 1953, June felt intuitively that it was Lady's time to give birth. She got up extra early before breakfast, before it was time to leave for school, to run out to Lady's stall in the barn. Nothing. No colt or filly. And she had been so certain that the new horse would appear that morning.

June went back in the house to eat breakfast, disappointed that she couldn't make the announcement that Lady's offspring had been delivered. Their father went out to finish chores while June and Brad got ready to leave for school.

Then, just before they drove off that morning, their father came running out of the barn to announce that a little filly had arrived. June was able to run to the barn and hug both Lady and the filly she christened Lucky and still not be late that morning for school.

Brad remembers that the summer of 1953 before he left for college, he saw his sister only at meals or when she helped with field work. Otherwise, she was with Lucky and Lady. June spent every spare moment currying the bodies of the mother and daughter, combing their manes and tails, talking to them, even singing to them. The family joked that June might as well sleep in the stall with the horses and learn to eat oats and hay.

Whenever he would come home from college on holidays, Brad would observe that June and Lucky seemed to have formed an incredible bond. He would watch in bemused wonder as June talked softly to Lucky and whispered in the filly's ear, as if the two of them shared some mysterious secret. It was both amusing and heartwarming to see June riding Lady with Lucky running behind, not wishing to be left out of the fun.

In April of 1955, June was a sophomore in high school, and Brad was a sophomore in college, home for Easter vacation. Their father decreed that the time had come when Lucky must be saddle broken. Who would do the honors?

Brad announced that he had no desire to be a bronc rider. He didn't want to be thrown from a bucking horse and arrive back at college with a broken arm or leg. He'd seen plenty of movies where the horse has a saddle thrown on its back for the first time and the rider is tossed about like a tiny boat in a big storm.

June looked away. She couldn't bear the thought of Lucky being frightened or hurt.

Their mother used to break horses when she was a girl, but those years were long past.

Their father, a husky, well-built man, volunteered for the job that he declared could not be put off any longer if the horse was ever going to be properly trained.

But their father was no fool, Brad said, recalling the event. He wasn't going to be laid up during spring farmwork. Four years before he had been thrown by a horse and was on his back during oats harvest. He said that he would take Lucky out on a field where there was soft, freshly plowed earth to cushion his fall in the event that he would be thrown. And, he allowed, that was quite likely.

So the family walked Lucky out to the plowed field. All the way, June was whispering to Lucky, telling her to be good to Dad, telling her that no one wanted to hurt her.

Their father threw the saddle on Lucky's back.
Lucky calmly turned inquisitively to look over her
shoulder. Next came the cinch around the middle.
Lucky seemed to be somewhat bewildered, just a little
uncomfortable, but she stood quietly, not moving a
muscle.

Then the family watched as Dad put a foot in
the stirrup and lifted himself into the saddle. Everyone said a silent prayer that he would not be hurt
when Lucky started bucking and kicking.

But Lucky seemed to have been waiting for that
moment to have someone on her back and to be
able to wear a saddle the way her mother, Lady, did.
Lucky did not buck; she did not kick. She merely
walked around the field, proudly, confidently. But
most of all, it was apparent that she wanted June to
sit in the saddle. Dad got off with a big smile and
began to laugh—partly, perhaps, out of relief for not
being tossed and thrown. But mostly out of surprise
and wonder.

June got in the saddle and rode Lucky for the rest
of the afternoon. She had shown the filly so much
love over the months that they had spent talking
and "whispering" together in the barn that Lucky
seemed to know exactly what was expected of her.
There was no need to buck and protest the moment
for which she had yearned so long. She wanted her

beloved friend June to be on her back, as well as in her heart.

That is why Brad says that his sister was a horse whisperer back in the 1950s. June had spent so much time and love on Lucky that the filly would do anything for her. If wearing a saddle on her back would mean that she and June would spend even more time together and explore more trails together, she wasn't going to object one bit. Over the months that June had spent talking in Lucky's stall and whispering in her ears, the two of them had entered a total mind linkup with one another and blended their spirits as one.

*W*e, the authors, have met very few horse owners who didn't feel that they could "talk" to their horses and that their animals could speak with them, either by mental telepathy or by a familiarity with the unique sounds and body language that the horse would use to indicate its messages.

In his book *Talking with Horses*, Henry Blake has created a kind of dictionary of forty-seven messages and fifty-four submessages connected with the sounds and signs that a horse might use to communicate with its owner. He also believes that when the owner has achieved a positive attitude toward the horse, extrasensory communication may be achieved.

Blake makes a very essential point in his book when he cautions all owners to always remember that horses are not humans. They must be respected and treated as the sovereign entities that they are.

"The greatest barrier to the understanding of any animal," Blake observes, "is anthropomorphism, that is to say, attributing human personality and behavior to animals."

Carole Devereux, author of *Spirit of the Horse*, theorizes that horses and humans once shared a psychic, spiritually based, nonverbal system of communication. Ms. Devereux firmly believes that there is evidence to support her theory in the Stone Age cave paintings of horses that were wrought during the last Ice Age. Furthermore, she maintains that the bond between humans and horses is a very special gift that can guide humanity on its spiritual quest.

After one of our lectures in which we were discussing the remarkable abilities of animals, Darrel Hardinger, nineteen, told us the following story of how a horse rescued him, as he put it, "from himself."

Darrel's childhood was an extremely difficult time for him. Shy and somewhat withdrawn, he explained that most of his early years he felt like a fish out of water. Complications from an illness at the age of four had depleted his immune system, leaving him weak. Advice from the family doctor to be extremely cautious with his health meant that Darrel couldn't take part in the normal physical activities of gym or sports at school—in fact, he had a "doctor's note" exempting him from strenuous exercise.

In spite of taking precautions, Darrel was still susceptible to every sniffle, cold, or flu that went around. Chicken pox hit him extra hard, and he contracted measles—*three* times! Allergies plagued him, so he was either stuffed up or sneezing with a runny nose. Kids picked on him and teased him incessantly. One of the insults a group of bullies said to him nearly every morning at school was, "You sound like you have a clothespin on your nose. Take it off, Snot Nose!"

Darrel blinked back tears even now as he recalled that "Snot Nose" had become his despised nickname in those early years. He could never understand how or why kids could be so cruel to one another.

"It's not like I wanted to be sick, I hated it," Darrel said. "I hated being called a 'sissy boy' even more!"

The more he tried to explain the doctor's admonition to be watchful for his health, the more the kids jeered at him. Each time he missed classes due to illnesses, he would get behind in his studies and rather than tutor or help him, the kids further accused him of being a slow learner—or worse, stupid. Darrel certainly didn't fit in with the athletes, nor could he claim membership in any clique of the popular kids in the band or choir, the students who concentrated on their studies, the civic-minded boys and girls in student government, or the guys and gals who concentrated on being cool. As his need and desire to be liked and understood grew daily more distant, Darrel became more and more withdrawn and very much a loner.

One day, Darrel's aunt Sarah, who was active in the local Humane Society, heard about an old horse that was no longer of any use to a local trail-ride camp. Circle Hills Ranch, a popular recreational facility for horseback riding, rented horses by the hour, day, or week to individuals or groups for supervised trail riding and camping. One of their horses, an old Appaloosa, had grown overweight, sluggish, and temperamental. Aunt Sarah said that she had been told they were going to dispose of the horse because it was simply too undependable and too much trouble. The whole Hardinger family had a love for animals—any and all animals—so they couldn't imagine that a good home couldn't be found for the horse. Actually, they had a thought that the horse might be good "therapy" for Darrel.

The rancher was so eager to get rid of the horse that he said the Hardingers could have it for free, and someone from Circle Hills would even deliver the animal to Darrel at the Hardinger farm.

Raider was the name the trail camp had given the horse. However, from the beginning of their relationship, Darrel stubbornly refused to dignify the sorry stallion by such nomenclature. Belligerently, he simply called him "Horse."

"It wasn't love at first sight," Darrel confessed. "I had such a chip on my shoulder. I guess I didn't even think a horse would like me, and I found myself treating him like the kids treated me at school . . . and that was terrible."

Describing the horse as ugly, fat, ornery, and somewhat swaybacked, Darrel said he begrudgingly learned how to care for and groom him, as he tried to make the best of the situation.

"My family all had such high hopes of how good this horse would be for me," Darrel said. "And the horse was a gift. So I tried to please them, and I often bit my tongue to keep from saying what I really thought about this useless horse."

Then one day, out of the blue, Darrel had a dramatic change of heart. He was just sitting on an old wooden box, feeling sorry for himself, when he heard the horse *talk* to him.

"I'd had a miserable day at school. Nothing I did was right, and even the teachers snapped at me," Darrel admitted. "I was feeling so depressed—to the point of having bad thoughts about life not being worth all this grief."

That was when Darrel heard "Horse" say, *"Nobody likes me. Why didn't they just put me out of my misery?"*

"Can you believe it?" Darrel asked us, laughing at the memory of that incredible moment. "I swear the horse was talking to me. I couldn't believe my ears."

Darrel went on to describe this as a pivotal moment in his entire life: "I realized that I was being a hypocrite by the way I was acting toward the horse. It suddenly dawned on me that the horse couldn't help it that it was getting older and not up to par for what the ranch expected of him. I was judging 'Horse' for being fat and slow, but was it his fault that he had arthritis and wasn't born a champion White Appaloosa with a pedigree of royalty? 'Horse' and I were alike. Two peas in a pod."

This transcendental experience at the age of fourteen had provided Darrel with the insight that there are some things in life that just don't seem fair, they *"just are."* Darrel didn't ask to be sickly; the horse didn't ask to get old and get dumped.

Acknowledging their mutual dilemma, Darrel blurted out in reply to the words he had heard from the horse, "Okay, you're right! I'm sorry!"

Darrel's comprehension of their shared "ill fate" in life caused him to rethink many of his actions toward "Horse," and from that moment on, a bond began to develop between them. Darrel began to show a different attitude toward his equine companion, starting by giving him a new name, a name that expressed their identity: *Lone Wolf.*

Darrel wasn't certain if his mind was playing tricks on him, or if Lone Wolf was a talking horse that could make him very wealthy. Each time Darrel perceived communication from Lone Wolf, he found himself studying the horse diligently.

"The horse's mouth didn't move—most of the time—but then other times, it actually appeared like it did," Darrel puzzled.

"Then, for my birthday, Aunt Sarah gave me your book, *Animal Miracles,*" Darrel told us. "I loved it! It was the first book I ever picked up to read that I simply couldn't put down, and I read it all over the weekend."

"It made me consider animals and, of course, my horse, in an entirely new way," Darrel said.

Pondering the possibility that he and Lone Wolf had a mystical telepathic bond, Darrel experimented with sending deliberate thoughts to his horse. It seemed to work. Darrel could tell that on days when he felt especially down, Lone Wolf reacted more sympathetically to him, as if to say, "It'll be okay, tell me about it."

"So, I found myself telling him everything," Darrel said. "I was spending so much time with my horse that my folks would often come out to see if I was all right, and in fact, I guess it would be fair to say nothing else interested me."

Darrell admitted to spending every waking moment, that wasn't in school, with Lone Wolf. "He just made me feel good. I felt safe with him," Darrel explained.

What had started as an occasional venting of emotions and frustration on particularly bad days, turned into a daily ritual of telling all. Every day Darrel would race home from school, eager to share his day with his best friend.

"I knew Lone Wolf could understand me, because he would lower his head, rest it gently on my shoulder—and rub against me now and then, assuring me that he was there for me," Darrel said.

"On one particular day when I didn't have much to say, and while I was cleaning out his stall, Lone Wolf did something pretty strange," Darrel puzzled.

Describing how his horse nudged him several times in the seat of the pants, although ever so lightly, Darrel said that the action took him off guard. "I got it that he was trying to tell me something, but I couldn't seem to get what it was, so I stopped spreading out the fresh hay, looked him in the eyes, told him to stop pushing me."

With that, Darrel "heard" Lone Wolf express a few complaints: "He wanted to be able to look outside on days when he was locked in the barn and he preferred a window or opening, facing north. And it didn't matter if the top half of the door was open and the elements blew in because he loved nature."

Darrel said he didn't question the reality of the horse's communication. "I saw exactly what Lone Wolf wanted as though he sent me a mental picture of his wish," Darrel told us. "I felt a little guilty, realizing all this time I'd been totally self-centered, thinking only of my own problems, and lost focus of how Lone Wolf felt."

Darrel didn't have to do more than to bring up the possibility of the slight remodeling in the barn to his dad, who offered to help with the endeavor.

"That is the first really good talk my dad and I ever had." Darrel beamed. While installing a north window/door and making a few other improvements to Lone Wolf's stall in the barn, another window of friendship opened between Darrel and his father, one that according to Darrel has continued to grow.

Subtle changes had occurred in Lone Wolf's personality, even before the "northern exposure." He was more cooperative, and often responded to Darrel's commands before they were uttered verbally, thereby astounding his parents with their son's horse-training abilities. Lone Wolf followed Darrel around the farm, more like a puppy dog than a horse, and soon they were inseparable.

The consistent grooming was giving Lone Wolf quite a healthy glow, according to Darrel. The daily quartering, as it is called, or brushing off the dirt and currying, as well as the more thorough grooming after exercise, called strapping, was paying off, and Lone Wolf was shaping up, filling out, firming up, and sporting a shining mane.

"The most miraculous changes, however, were those in my own life," Darrel told us. "It took me a couple of years to piece everything together, but now there is no question in my mind that Lone Wolf was the best psychiatrist, the best doctor, the best friend I could have ever had. The unconditional love of a horse that I once thought of as ugly—and that others thought of as dispensable—gave me the will to go on. Lone Wolf was the best thing that ever happened to me."

Darrel emphasized that not only did his health change from his always being ill to rarely being sick at all, but also the attitude of his fellow classmates went from jeering to cheering. "Maybe it was because

Lone Wolf took the chip off my shoulder and gave me his broad shoulders and together we transcended the woes of not feeling wanted or loved," Darrel said. "So many people have told me I'm a different person—in a positive way."

In concluding his touching and inspirational story, Darrel said that now and then someone will ask him what brought about such a dramatic change in his life. Darrel told us that he can't help saying, "It was an ugly, useless horse that taught me how to live."

Darrel's life was so inspired by his deep relationship with his horse that he made a commitment to someday open a horse-riding facility where he will be able to help others. He plans to pursue a degree in child psychology to complement his love and acquired skills in caring for and training horses. The focus would be to work with troubled children, offering what Darrel has learned from his own life experiences regarding how important it is to be needed and loved. Because Darrel intends to demonstrate all of this through the magical bond of horse and human, he plans to call his facility the Lone Wolf Center.

The horse's gift as psychotherapist is coming to be appreciated by many. In her article, "The Healing Horse," freelance equine journalist Kate Hester tells how horses are being used in programs for drug addicts, prisoners, and troubled children and teens. In *Natural Horse* magazine, Volume 3, Issue 6, 2001, Ms. Hester writes that riding therapy is being used very successfully not only to help people with learning disabilities but also to benefit those with mental-health problems. "Riders often develop a bond with the horse that alleviates feelings of loneliness, depression and isolation," she states.

The commanding size and weight of a 1,300-pound horse—big and strong, coupled with the warmth of their living personalities, completely nonjudgmental and without condemnation—make for an extraordinary therapist!

The acknowledged therapeutic, psychotherapeutic benefits of the horse go way back, as long ago as 435–354 B.C.E., when it is recorded that Xenophon wrote, "The horse is a good master not only for the body, but also for the mind and the heart."

Hippocrates, the wise old Greek physician, insisted that the injured and the ill recovered sooner if they rode on horseback. He also indicated that there was a psychological effect of horseback riding that could assist those individuals suffering from melancholy or depression to free themselves from dark thoughts and to create more cheerful ones.

Therapeutic riding differs from hippotherapy, the use of a horse by trained therapists for assisting the disabled in a controlled environment to achieve functional outcomes such as improved neurological function and sensory processing. Therapeutic riding refers primarily to the positive mental and emotional benefits that can be derived from horseback riding, such as those in the building of self-confidence, self-esteem, self-awareness. The simple joy and freedom that come from the recreational aspect of riding a horse may be considered as well, of course.

Sixty-one-year-old Alba Mae J. encountered a series of losses in her life that left her so depressed she found she could barely function. Telling us that she didn't remember a time in her entire life when she didn't bounce right back from any disappointment or malady, she confessed that the last two events were like extra weights that tipped the scale to the other side and she couldn't find her balance.

Alba's husband, who'd never been sick a day in his life, passed away suddenly of a heart attack. Since he had no history of a heart problem, his death came as a total shock to Alba, and she was still in denial. In addition, she was still grieving over the death of her brother, who only eight months before her husband's passing had been killed in a car accident, the fault of a drunk driver.

Alba told us that her friends and neighbors, who had known her most of her life, were aware of a number of difficult situations that she triumphantly faced in her past, so they became quite concerned for her well-being when, after two years, she was not bouncing back from the deaths of her brother and husband.

"Nearly catatonic, I refused to take part in activities or social events of any kind," Alba said. "It was all I could do to go to the grocery store." Then one day, Alba's niece literally dragged her to accompany her to a nearby horse stable. Not certain if it was deliberate calculating on the part of her niece, who knew that as a girl, Alba loved horses, or if it was sheer coincidence, Alba said, "It was my ticket to sanity."

Alba explained that she found herself mysteriously drawn to Fandango, one of the horses in the stable, who reminded her of her old pal, "Skrogins," a horse she'd had when she was a young girl. Skrogins was fatally injured in a fall, but he had been her best friend for ten years.

"I simply felt a little peace of mind when I gazed upon this particular horse, so I set out to see him again," Alba said.

Fandango provoked the first happy feeling Alba had experienced in years, and she confessed that she wasn't even certain that she wanted to feel happy. To her great concern, she realized that she'd had grown so used to the gnawing emptiness that she didn't really know if she wanted to disturb it.

"Late in the evening, when no one else was around, I just stood there, sometimes for what seemed like hours, staring at Fandango and talking to him," Alba said.

For months, Alba was able to visit her newfound friend unnoticed, as she unburdened her soul to this patient, kind horse. Fandango had become so accustomed and attuned to Alba's feelings that many times she was positive that she saw tears of sympathy well up in the horse's eyes.

Fandango's owner came by one evening, completely taking Alba by surprise, but he tried to assure her that he didn't mind at all if she took a liking to his horse. In fact, he offered her a part-time job in the stables, helping out with the horses.

Alba told us that the horse had to be an angel. "Fandango knew the days I was extra blue," Alba said. "He'd put his head down and rest it on my shoulder until he seemed to know it was too heavy for me, then he'd move it to the other shoulder for a little while. Fandango gave me unconditional love and the opportunity to express my hurt and pain in a way that was safe and healing."

Alba smiled as she continued: "That little glimmer of peace that I didn't really want to feel in the first place has deepened; and as the heavy weight of buckets of tears flowed out of me, there began to be room for joy in my life again."

Alba explained that there would always be a feeling of loneliness and a void left by the loss of her beloved husband and partner of so many years, and that nothing could ever replace her husband and her brother, but at least now she knew that she could carry on. "Fandango seemed to know and understand me, as he stood guard over and near me—as psychotherapist/minister/healer—and my life was given back to me," she said.

Alba enjoys introducing others to the wonders of horses and the patient, empathetic help they offer.

"Horses may be the best therapists around. Soon I might even put a plaque below Fandango's name-plate that reads: *Certified Horse Psychotherapist,*" Alba joked.

*A*fter trying everything imaginable to
ease the severe migraine headaches that
disabled him most of his life, thirty-seven-year-old
Mason Sandusky was cured by a horse. Years ago,
Mason was diagnosed with chronic, intractable
migraine syndrome, and in an effort to find relief, he
spent a great deal of his time in doctors' offices. The
headaches were so unbearable, Mason said, he should
have had his own revolving door in the emergency
room of the local hospital, because that is where he
seemed to be spending all of his time.

While in the waiting room during one of his hospital visits, he struck up a conversation with a "fellow sufferer," who asked Mason if he'd heard about a
new therapy that some of the nurses were discussing.
The man told Mason that a nurse had mentioned a

program that had been fairly successful with several migraine patients and it involved riding horses.

"We both laughed like fools, but at least the laugh temporarily lessened our pain," Mason explained. "After all, with all the thousands of dollars we'd spent on medicine and doctors—clinical trials, even—how was bouncing around on a horse's back going to help our headaches?"

But later, in the grip of painful desperation, Mason decided to find out more about horse therapy. He enrolled in a program and found it so helpful that he soon bought his own horse.

"I don't know how to explain it, but now I'm down to having at the most several episodes this year, and to me that is a miracle!" Mason said. "Bouncing around on a horse sounded like torture to a man with a migraine, but I'm not laughing now."

Now that he has learned through this unusual therapy that horses can become miracle-workers with troubled children and adults with behavioral and learning disorders, as well as with those suffering from depression and migraines, Mason has a new ambition. He hopes to start his own therapeutic horse camp, "for anyone with headaches of any kind or origin."

*P*erhaps the greatest racehorse in the Olympus of track legends is Kincsem, a filly from Hungary, who, from the time she began racing at the age of two until she retired at a mature five years old, won all fifty-four of her races. Kincsem, whose name is Hungarian for "My Treasure," proved to be a literal treasure trove for her owner, Ernst von Blaskovitch, from her first race on June 21, 1876, until her last on October 21, 1879.

In 1876, at age two, Kincsem had ten starts and ten wins; in 1877, at age three, seventeen starts and seventeen wins; in 1878, at age four, fifteen starts and fifteen wins; and in 1879, at age five, twelve starts and twelve wins. The fantastic filly raced triumphantly across the Continent and defeated the best horses that Europe and the United Kingdom had to offer. She became the pride of Hungary and the toast of all of Europe.

Many race enthusiasts commented on Kincsem's peculiar racing style. She would run most of the race with her head lowered, as if scanning the track for bits of grass on which to nibble while her challengers tried to match her pace. Often, she would appear to give the pack of her competitors a bit of a head start, then quickly catch up to the bunch and handily pass them all to come in ahead by several lengths at the finish line.

Foaled in 1874 by Water Nymph and sired by Cambuscan, the chestnut filly triumphed at such races as the Magyar One and Two Thousand Guines Stakes in Hungary, the Preis der Jockey Club and the Emperor's Prize in Austria, the Grosser Preis van Baden-Baden (three times) in Germany, the Gran Prix de Deauville in France, and the Goodwood Cup in England.

Kincsem produced five foals and died at the age of thirteen in 1887 while she was giving birth to a filly named Kincs, who would later foal Napfeny, a future winner of the Magyar Oaks. Napfeny would foal Miczi, who carried on Kincsem's tradition of triumphs by coming in first at the Magyar Oaks, the Nemzeti-Hafiazi Prize, the Osterreichisches Stutenpries, the Queen Elizabeth Prize, and the King's Prize. In spite of many wars in Europe—including the First and Second World Wars—since Kincsem died in 1887, her bloodline, while depleted, was not destroyed. In the late 1950s, two of Kincsem's descendents, Wald-canter and Wicht, were considered among the best of Europe's champion racehorses.

*I*n 1997, we heard about Gail Claussen, a rancher in Rush, Colorado, who, though almost totally blind, still managed to ride herd on his 3,000-acre spread with the help of Silk Shotgun, his "seeing-eye" horse. After many years of ranching, Claussen, sixty, found that he suffered from macular degeneration, a genetic condition that caused blood clots to form on the retinas of his eyes. When he would ride out to check on his horses, he could only perceive them as shadowy blurs on the range.

That was when Claussen thanked his lucky stars for Silk Shotgun, his big quarter horse stallion, who knew from many years' experience and instinct exactly what to do when he headed out to check the herd. Just by the way the horse held himself, Claussen told writer Nick Isenberg, he could tell whether Silk Shotgun was encountering another horse, a calf, or a badger.

Claussen also had full confidence in letting the horse go "full bore" without worrying that he would step in a hole or stumble in a dip in the pasture. Somehow, the trusty Silk Shotgun was able to keep one eye on the herd and another watching out for hazardous terrain.

The powerfully built quarter horse expertly drives the herd of 100 black Angus cattle toward the corrals, separating the cows from the calves as they near the pens. Once the cattle are separated, Claussen's wife, Karol, gives the adults a healthy dose of fly spray. If any of the cows should decide that they want to skip out on the clouds of smelly spray, Silk Shotgun gives them a quick nip on their rear quarters to convince them to undergo the ordeal.

When Claussen first learned that he was going blind in 1991, he underwent a rather dark period of depression. But once he realized that Silk Shotgun's skills and devotion and Karol's love and support would always be there to help compensate for his loss of sight, Claussen told Isenberg that he felt "good about everything."

*C*omanche, a tough mustang that had already been wounded in a number of skirmishes as a cavalry officer's horse, was the sole survivor of the defeat of General George A. Custer's command at the Battle of the Little Bighorn (famously known as "Custer's Last Stand") on June 25, 1876. Although Comanche never again carried a cavalryman in his saddle, he participated in formal regimental functions until he died on November 7, 1891.

Comanche began his life running free on the open range as a member of a mustang herd. When he was about four years old, he was captured by cowboys in a wild horse roundup, gelded, and sold to the U.S. Army Cavalry on April 3, 1862. Captain Myles Keogh took a fancy to the reddish brown mustang, and Comanche soon became Keogh's favorite battle charger. At 925 pounds, about sixty inches high, the tough-as-leather mustang carried the captain into many military actions and had been wounded twelve times as a result of close combat.

Since Comanche was the only member of Custer's battalion of the Seventh Regiment of the U.S. Cavalry that survived the defeat at the Little Bighorn, historians will never know exactly what battle plan General Custer sought to employ on that fateful day in June 1876. There is a consensus among most historians who have tried to reconstruct the events of that day that Custer disobeyed the orders of General Alfred Terry and divided the Seventh Cavalry Regiment of 650 men into three battalions under the command of Major Reno, Captain Benteen, and himself. It is also generally agreed that Custer ignored his scouts' reports that there were thousands of Indians from at least six tribes encamped on the Little Bighorn River. Whether due to his own arrogance or a fatal misinterpretation of the enormity of the forces gathered against him, Custer decided not to wait for support from Reno and Benteen and chose to attack what he believed to be the middle of the encampment on the central ford of the Little Bighorn with his battalion of 196 men. Estimates of the combined tribal forces suggest that Custer and his battalion found themselves confronting more than 2,500 warriors from the Cheyenne, Sans Arcs,

Miniconjoux Sioux, Oglala Sioux, Hunkpapa Sioux, and Blackfeet tribes. Some historians have further estimated that the total number of the tribespeople in the massive encampment may have been as high as 15,000. In less than twenty minutes, Custer and his troopers were annihilated to the last man.

Two days after the defeat of Custer's battalion of the Seventh Cavalry, a burial party found Comanche standing alone in a thicket near the battle scene. He had seven arrows in his body, but the indomitable horse was still alive.

With great care approaching reverence for the sole survivor of the greatest defeat the U.S. Army had ever suffered at the hands of the Plains Indians, Comanche was transported by steamboat to Fort Lincoln 950 miles away. Once safely delivered to the Seventh Cavalry Post, the seemingly indestructible horse was allowed to spend the next year recuperating from his wounds.

For the next twelve years, Comanche remained at Fort Lincoln where he enjoyed a special status as a kind of symbol of the fighting spirit of the Seventh Cavalry. Orders were issued that Comanche was never again to be ridden even for the most routine duties. At formal regiment functions, he was draped in black, stirrups and boots reversed, and led at the head of the company.

In 1888, Comanche was transferred with the Seventh Cavalry to Fort Riley, Kansas, where he continued to serve as a symbol of the tragic defeat at the Little Bighorn. When he died of colic on November 7, 1891, officers of the Seventh Cavalry requested that Lewis Lindsay Dyche of the University of Kansas mount Comanche's remains. Today, the earthly shell of the mustang that survived Custer's Last Stand can be seen at the University of Kansas Museum of Natural History, Dyche Hall, Lawrence, Kansas.

*B*lack Jack, a beautiful black gelding, was the last horse issued to the U.S. Army by the quartermaster, and he was the last to bear the "U.S." brand on his hide. Born on January 19, 1947, of uncertain breeding, Black Jack was named for General John J. "Black Jack" Pershing, Supreme Commander of the American Expeditionary Force in World War I.

Pershing's horse in that military action was Kidron, the proud steed that the general rode triumphantly through the Victory Arch in New York City at the end of the war in 1918. In World War I, 6 million horses served as cavalry mounts or draft animals for the American forces in Europe. Nearly all of them were killed. The American Expeditionary Force brought with them an additional 182,000 horses to the war zones. Of these valiant battle chargers, only 200 came back home to the United States.

The day of the mounted cavalry charge and the effectiveness of the horse in warfare ended with the barbed wire, machine guns, and trenches of World War I. By the end of that bloody conflict, the horse population of the United States and Europe was significantly reduced in number.

While Black Jack never carried a soldier into battle, from 1953 to 1973 he served the Army as a riderless horse in ceremonial functions and solemn funeral processions. In the thousands of funeral processions in which Black Jack participated at Arlington National Cemetery, he was the caparisoned riderless horse that followed the flag-covered coffin, with boots reversed in the stirrups, a symbol of the fallen hero.

In November 1963, millions of television viewers around the world saw the stately black horse prancing behind the flag-draped casket of President John F. Kennedy as the fallen leader was borne to Arlington National Cemetery. Black Jack was also the riderless horse in the funeral processions of President Herbert Hoover (1964), General Douglas MacArthur (1964), and President Lyndon B. Johnson (1973).

Black Jack entered semiretirement in 1973 and died on February 6, 1976, at the age of twenty-nine. The ashes of the last U.S. Army horse were placed in an urn at his monument at Fort Meyer, Virginia.

When horse owner Mary Lynn Whiten first met Levi at the stable where her daughter took riding lessons, he was horribly thin and starving. Mary Lynn told writer Kimberley Freeman that no one would ride him because he was considered mean, and angry.

"The stable owner planned to sell him to 'the meat man' and I intervened," she told Kimberley. "I struck a monthly payment deal and ate fried egg sandwiches for over a year to make payments and board fees. But Levi soon repaid me many times over."

Mary Lynn explained that at the time she was in an abusive eleven-year marriage. "One day, for some reason, Levi decided to jump a huge gully," she said. "On the way over, I looked down and thought to myself, 'This is suicide.' Once safely on the other side, I thought to myself, 'My marriage is suicide. This is just life.' I filed for divorce the next day."

After several years, Mary Lynn told Kimberley, she and Levi reached a place in their relationship where they didn't need to think or talk. "We moved fluidly together in the saddle and on the ground," Mary Lynn recalled. "In the evenings, Levi would put his head over my shoulder and pull me in to him for a hug. We'd just sit still and quiet, simply being together."

In the following year, Mary Lynn had a severe reaction to an antibiotic, Biaxin. Her joints from the waist down were inflamed and her muscles were in a continuous spasm. "I could only walk on my toes, and I cried at every step," she said. "Levi helped me every day when I took him to and from his paddock. He would walk slowly next to me with his neck lowered, letting me hang by myself over him in order to relieve the weight on my feet. I wish he could have escorted me everywhere."

Once when Levi became colicky and his intestines were in knots, Mary Lynn told Kimberley, she held Levi's head in her lap and sang to him as they waited for the vet to arrive. "I told Levi that if something bad happened and we were separated, he should always look for me," she said. "I told him that I would always look for him and that we would find each other again. For the next two years, whenever his health condition became serious, that's what I'd tell him."

Mary Lynn said that Levi made her realize how connected humans can be to the other creatures on this Earth. When Levi was sick, she "took on" his sickness. "I could feel it," she explained to Kimberley. "Levi would have a symptom and I'd take it on and share it with him. I could tell the vet where he was hurting because I could feel it in my own body."

At thirty years old, Levi contracted peritonitis and was admitted to the University of Georgia (UGA) clinic. They told Mary Lynn that her horse was too old and that his usefulness was over. They said that it was time to put him down.

"There was no way I was going to give up like that, much less part with my dear friend," Mary Lynn recalled. "My response was, 'Do whatever it takes. Here's my empty Visa card, fill it up.'"

She spent the next year visiting Levi every day at the clinic. The veterinarian-technicians said that Levi knew that Mary Lynn was there as soon as she turned the corner to his aisle.

In December, a lump developed on the left side of Levi's head. The diagnosis was cancer—a squamous-cell carcinoma—and Mary Lynn spent another year going back and forth to UGA. Four radiation treatments and continuous follow-up visits later, the cancer seemed to be slowing down and Levi came home.

"A year later, during a routine vet exam, they found a hole in Levi's colon," Mary Lynn recalled sadly. "I had no choice; I had to put down my best friend or watch him die in misery within days.

"Levi passed at thirty-four," she told Kimberley Freeman, concluding her story. "We'd been together for twenty-four of these years, during which he was my best friend and dearest soulmate. He will always be my shining example of how a horse can give you hope, open your mind, and change your life."

Shamanism

*I*n recent years, there has been a rising interest in the shamanism and the lore of Native American medicine ways and traditional religion. More and more men and women are interested in learning about totem animals and medicine wheel symbols.

Some years ago, our friend Sun Bear, a Chippewa medicine man who founded the Bear Tribe, the first new tribe of the twentieth century, explained to us about the medicine wheel cosmology that he had realized through his visions and had expressed with the assistance of his medicine helper, Wabun. The Great Mystery had revealed to him a Native American zodiac, complete with representative totem animals.

Many readers who respond to the colorful and dynamic symbols of American Indian medicine may like to know how to determine their horse's (and maybe their own) totem power animal. Simply find the birthday of your horse below and study the implications for a better relationship between you and your equine companion. Some people have given their horses a name based on the totem animal in order to increase its opportunity to achieve a better balance on the Earth Mother. Remember, to the Native Americans all life is one—and your horse may receive energy from a power symbol just as much as you can.

The Red Hawk—March 19 to April 19
Those born under the Native American zodiacal sign of the Red Hawk are likely to be adventurous and assertive. They cherish a desire to be free, and those closest to them may sometimes consider them a bit headstrong.

The Beaver—April 20 to May 20
Those of the Beaver sign are generally blessed with good health. They cherish peace and security, and they are thought by all to be loyal and stable.

The Deer—May 21 to June 21
Clever and talented entities are found under the sign of the Deer. Your Deer horse will exhibit a generally

positive disposition and will sometimes appear to be a creature of perpetual motion.

The Brown Flicker—June 22 to July 21

Entities born under this sign have a strong nesting instinct and are usually deemed to be good parents. Brown Flicker beings love peace and quiet and seek to avoid serious conflicts.

The Sturgeon—July 22 to August 21

Sturgeon beings have a great ability to teach others. They may be considered a bit domineering, but they generally bring a positive approach to every problem.

The Bear—August 22 to September 22

Entities born under this sign of the Native American zodiac are usually slow, cautious, and quiet. Your horse companion born under the sign of the Bear is probably a no-nonsense animal that seems to be able to detect insincerity in others.

The Raven—September 23 to October 22

Raven beings are sociable and energetic, full of nervous energy and fluctuating moods. They are generally very flexible and adapt well to new environments and circumstances.

The Snake—October 23 to November 21

Charismatic but often difficult to comprehend, Snake entities often present a problem to those around them. Beings born under the sign of the Snake may hide a deceptive nature behind a charming exterior.

The Elk—November 22 to December 21

Elk beings are competitive and athletic, but they are also patient and kind. Entities born under the sign of the Elk enjoy a change of scene every now and then—and cherish a strong independent streak.

The Snow Goose—December 22 to January 20

If your horse companion was born under the sign of the Snow Goose, you have a friend that is content to stay at your side and that generally shows little interest in any dramatic alterations of the daily routine. Far from sluggish, however, the creature born under the sign of the Snow Goose has great stamina.

The Otter—January 21 to February 18

Otter beings are often regarded as unpredictable and mercurial. If your horse was born under the sign of the Otter, you will have a companion that will generally be good-natured and a loyal friend.

The Cougar—February 19 to March 18

Cougar beings are mystical. You will probably experience some fascinating telepathic link with your Cougar horse. Watch your tone of voice and your nonverbal communication as well, for those born under this sign are very sensitive and easily hurt by disapproval or rejection.

*S*eabiscuit was a loser who rose from obscurity to become the most famous racehorse of his day. In 1938, Walter Winchell, an influential and popular columnist, named Seabiscuit one of the top ten newsmakers of the year, right up there with Franklin Delano Roosevelt, the president of the United States, and Adolf Hitler, chancellor of Germany. In the midst of a national depression that had demoralized the entire nation, a runty, knobby-kneed racehorse with crooked legs inspired the American people to summon the necessary optimism to pull themselves out of a terrible economic slump and beat the odds.

Seabiscuit competed in eighty-nine races, running competitively until he was seven years old, finishing at the top of his game at a much older age than the average racehorse does. When he was a two-year-old, Seabiscuit started in thirty-five races and won only five of them. The next year, he won nine out of twenty-three races, before he was acquired by Charles and Marcella Howard in a claiming race for $7,500.

When Howard turned Seabiscuit over to his trainer, Tom Smith, the horse was 200 pounds underweight, suffering from fatigue and stress, and possessed of a fearful temperament that intimidated both racetrack personnel and the other horses. Smith was an old cowboy who truly loved horses. He could understand how a three-year-old horse that had been raced fifty-eight times in two years could be feeling the strain of physical exhaustion. Smith set about providing Seabiscuit with some tender, loving care and with a special diet to put some flesh back on his bones. He wrapped the horse's legs with bandages and gave him a double-sized stall, complete with bunkmates—Pocatell, a stray dog; Jo-Jo, a spider monkey; and Pumpkin, a tranquil horse that would be Seabiscuit's traveling companion. In addition, Smith introduced the horse to Johnny "Red" Pollard, an ex-boxer, who would be Seabiscuit's jockey. Pollard and the racehorse bonded quickly, and the jockey nicknamed Seabiscuit, "Pops."

The three men—Smith, Howard, and Pollard—transformed the once skittish, underweight, and terrible-tempered horse into a relaxed, easygoing, sturdy animal. Their strategy was to begin running Seabiscuit in small allowance races and build up his strength and endurance. By the end of 1936, Seabiscuit had won the Scarsdale Handicap and two major races in California, narrowly missing setting two world records.

Seabiscuit began his four-year-old season in 1937 by winning his first race of the year at Santa Anita. Later, running confidently in the Santa Anita Handicap, Seabiscuit was surprised by Rosemont with one furlong to go, and he lost by a nose in a photo finish. In spite of that disappointing loss, Seabiscuit went on to race in seven states that year, crossing the finish line victoriously in ten major races. The knobby-kneed wonder was gaining national attention, tying five track records and becoming the year's leading money winner. In spite of Seabiscuit's increasing popularity among racing fans, the glory that year went to War Admiral, the Triple Crown winner.

Shortly before Seabiscuit began his five-year-old season by racing in the Santa Anita Derby, Pollard was injured and put out of commission for a year. George Woolf, a friend of Pollard's and an acclaimed jockey, assumed the saddle atop Seabiscuit. Woolf rode Seabiscuit to a neck-and-neck finish at the wire, but Stagehand managed to finish first.

The Santa Anita loss didn't seem to matter to racing fans, who demanded a duel on the track between the sleek War Admiral, the Triple Crown winner, and the little underdog Seabiscuit. Belmont Park offered a $100,000 purse in May of 1938 for a match race between the two thoroughbreds. Charles Howard accepted the challenge. He was eager to pit Seabiscuit against the winner of the Kentucky Derby, the Preakness Stakes, and the Belmont Stakes. However, that face-off and a subsequent race at Suffolk Downs in June never occurred, because of an injury to Seabiscuit's legs.

Red Pollard began training again that summer, and he hoped that he would be in shape in time to ride Seabiscuit in any match that might be set against War Admiral. It seemed that both Pollard and Pops were ill-fated regarding their legs, for the jockey had no sooner begun riding again when the colt he was working out crashed into the side of a barn and the resulting accident nearly severed Pollard's leg. A team of doctors informed the hospitalized jockey that it was unlikely that he would ever walk again.

On November 1, 1938, the race of the decade was set between Seabiscuit and War Admiral at Pimlico Racecourse. While the smart money bet on War Admiral to break away at the starting gate and leave

Seabiscuit in the dust, what they didn't know was that the old cowboy Tom Smith had been clanging a starting bell in their training sessions and conditioning Seabiscuit to speed away at the beginning of the race. Smith had also teamed Seabiscuit with horses that were trained to sprint, thereby challenging him to start off at full throttle to catch them.

In addition to the spectators that packed the stands on November 1, it has been estimated that another 40 million people listened to the race on the radio. At the sound of the bell, Seabiscuit shot off to a two-length lead. At the half-mile pole, War Admiral pounded up to run shoulder to shoulder with Seabiscuit, but the older horse would not yield to the younger challenger. Seabiscuit won by four lengths, crossing the finish line in near world-record time.

In January 1939, Seabiscuit's six-year-old season, his left front tendon finally ruptured, and he was sent to Charles Howard's Ridgewood Ranch to recuperate. The word in the racing world was that Seabiscuit had retired. And why shouldn't he? He had already entered more races than nearly any other racehorse in the history of racing. He had won Horse of the Year in 1938. Why not leave when he was a champion?

While Seabiscuit wandered the pastures at Ridgewood Ranch, he was joined by his old friend,

Red Pollard, who had undergone numerous surgeries on his leg and was able to walk on crutches. Pollard began to ride Pops and recondition him. By the end of the year, the jockey had convinced Howard that Seabiscuit was ready for a comeback. Tom Smith agreed that nine months of training had brought their champion back to winning form.

Incredibly, in 1940, Pollard put on a steel leg brace and rode the seven-year-old horse in the Santa Anita Handicap. Seabiscuit was more than twice the age of the horses that gathered at the starting gate. A crowd of 70,000 fans filled the stands that day to see if the impossible would be accomplished.

For a few tense moments, Pollard and Pops seemed to be trapped in a pocket behind the pack of youngsters. And then Seabiscuit thundered ahead and won the handicap with the second fastest mile and a quarter in American racing history.

After this remarkable victory, it really was time to retire. In his six years of racing, Seabiscuit had started in eighty-nine events, won thirty-three of them, and set sixteen track records. On May 17, 1947, at fourteen years of age, Seabiscuit died of a heart attack at Ridgewood Ranch.

*I*n the early days of June 2003, an underdog racing horse named Funny Cide captured the hearts of millions of men, women, and children who love with equal enthusiasm both horses and a rags-to-riches success story. After Funny Cide had won the Kentucky Derby and the Preakness, he became the even-money favorite to win the Belmont Stakes and become the first Triple Crown champion since Affirmed claimed that title in 1978. If Funny Cide were to cross the finish line before his chief rival, Empire Maker, did, he would become the first gelding ever to win the Triple Crown.

Funny Cide was born on April 20, 2000, at McMahon of Saratoga Thoroughbred Farm, Saratoga, New York. Originally purchased by Tony Everard, Funny Cide was sold on March 2002 for $75,000 to the Sackatoga Stable, a group composed of six high school friends and four other investors from Saratoga Springs, New York. Funny Cide was brought by Sackatoga Stable into the competent hands of trainer Barclay Tagg, a former steeplechase jockey, and his assistant Robin Smullen. Funny Cide's jockey since August 2002 has been Jose Santos.

In his maiden races on September 8 and September 29, Funny Cide won by fifteen lengths and nine lengths, respectively. On October 19, at Sleepy Hollow Race Track, Funny Cide managed to win by a neck, but in his race at the Holy Bull Stakes on January 18, 2003, he finished in fifth place. At the Louisiana Derby in March, he managed to finish third, though his place was later moved to second because of the disqualification of Kafwain.

Few racing fans were impressed with Funny Cide's record, but at the Wood Memorial on April 12, he finished in second place, losing to Empire Maker by a mere half length.

In the days before the Kentucky Derby, Funny Cide was not considered a serious challenge to the field. Experts groused that the gelding's three victories had been against fellow New York–bred horses. Funny Cide just didn't have the right stuff to compete on the Louisville, Kentucky, track.

Then, on May 3, Funny Cide became the first gelding since Clyde Van Dusen in 1929 to win the

Kentucky Derby. He was also the first New York–bred horse ever to win the coveted Derby crown. In addition, he beat Empire Maker and the clock to finish at 2:01.19, the tenth-fastest time in Derby history.

At the Preakness Stakes on May 17, Funny Cide became the thirty-first Kentucky Derby champion to cross the finish line ahead of the pack and win the second goal of the Triple Crown. Funny Cide became the seventh gelding to win the Preakness Stakes, and he triumphed by 9¾ lengths, the second-largest margin in Preakness history.

No one was laughing at Funny Cide after his victories at the Kentucky Derby and the Preakness Stakes. For the Belmont Stakes, the third jewel in racing's most coveted crown, he would face five challengers on a 1½-mile track. His jockey, Jose Santos, conceding that anything could happen, expressed his confidence that they would win.

The prerace excitement preceding the Belmont Stakes had not been felt throughout the general public for many years. The horse had become the people's horse, a favorite with the fans and with those individuals who never paid much attention to the world of racing and horses. School children wrote letters to Funny Cide. New Yorkers, especially, were keyed up to cheer their equine hero to victory.

Hours before the race began on June 7, a steady downpour soaked the track and turned the turf into mud. Officials had estimated a record crowd of more than 120,000 fans, but far fewer than that number braved the rain to sit in the stands with umbrellas and racing programs to prevent them from getting sopping wet.

Funny Cide started fast and led the other five horses onto the muddy track, but he couldn't maintain the advantage. With three-eighths of a mile to go, Empire Maker charged forward with a burst of speed that Funny Cide could not match. Empire Maker came in first; Ten Most Wanted, second; and Funny Cide crossed the line in third place.

As Funny Cide was being led off the track, the crowd gave him several rousing cheers. Although he had lost the Belmont Stakes, the horse that came from nowhere had won the Kentucky Derby and the Preakness Stakes. He will go down in racing history as a champion.

For many generations, children have thrilled to Longfellow's stirring poem that tells of Paul Revere's midnight ride to alert the patriots of Lexington that the British troops were about to invade the countryside. Paul Revere, a goldsmith and courier, has become immortalized for riding from Boston to Lexington to contact patriot leaders Samuel Adams and John Hancock and warn them about the coming invasion. Revere's successful fulfillment of his mission proved to be a turning point in the American War of Independence.

On the evening of April 8, 1775, Revere saw the signal of two lanterns shining in the tower of Christ Church and got into the boat with men who were waiting to bring him across the river to Charlestown. In his account of his dangerous ride, Revere stated that he borrowed a very fine mare from a

231

merchant named John Larkin. When Revere arrived in Lexington after completing his mission, he and two other patriots were captured by a British patrol. Revere was in no position to protest when a British sergeant confiscated the horse that he had ridden to sound the alarm.

The mare was never seen again by Revere or by John Larkin. There would have been no famous ride of Paul Revere and no warning spread to the patriots without the participation of a fast horse. How can it be that we don't even know the name of one of the most famous horses in American history?

Searching for the mare's identity is made even harder by the fact that most people in Colonial days did not give their equine companions individual names. However, Patrick M. Leehey, of the Paul Revere Memorial Association, Boston, provides a likely identification of the horse that helped warn the patriots on that fateful night in 1775. In 1930, the descendents of John Larkin, the merchant who provided the mare to Revere, published a family genealogy in which it is recorded that Samuel Larkin (1701–1784), a chair maker and fisherman who had horses and a stable, was requested by his son John to loan his mare Brown Beauty to Paul Revere.

While there is no other historical evidence to corroborate the famous horse's identity, Brown

Beauty seems an appropriate name for the swift mare that helped to spread the alarm of a forthcoming invasion to the patriots of colonial Massachusetts.

*W*hen Brad Steiger was a boy, he knew that his father would let old Dan live out his retirement years grazing peacefully in the pasture until the draft horse was called home to the Great Corral in the sky. Brad had heard the story many times about Dan saving his father's life when he got lost in a blizzard.

Brad was born in the big blizzard of 1936. All his life he has heard tales about what a big storm that was. Brad heard how his mother and he had to remain for a couple of weeks in the Fort Dodge Lutheran Hospital and how they had to stay in the house in town with Grandpa and Grandma and how they couldn't get home to Dad on the farm for a month. Although February 1936 may have been the Granddaddy of All Blizzards, if you are out on the prairies alone and a blinding whiteout with strong, howling winds catches you, you can be in just as much trouble and freeze just as fast even if the storm isn't one for the record books.

In those days, when a snowstorm descended upon the hinterlands, folks out on the farms could be snowbound for weeks. If the farm families should be caught short of supplies, those weeks could pass very slowly.

On the occasion of this particular winter's storm in 1938, it had already begun snowing rather hard when Brad's father decided that he must hitch Dan to the wagon and go into town for some groceries, kerosene, and fuel oil. His keen weather eye advised him that enough snow could fall in the next couple of days to block the roads, so he set out on the gravel road that would take him the three miles to town. There was no electricity in their home at that time, so Brad's father could not hear the weather bulletin that was interrupting regularly scheduled radio broadcasts to warn people to beware of the fast-approaching blizzard.

By the time Brad's father left town with the loaded wagon for the return trip to the farm, the heavily falling snow was nearing whiteout conditions. Although the clerks in the grocery store warned him to be cautious and advised him of the increasing ferocity of the storm, they knew that he would not think of taking refuge in town and leaving his wife and infant son huddled around the cookstove in the kitchen. Besides, he had Dan with him. It wasn't as if he were heading out into the storm alone.

The entire clan would be everlastingly grateful to Dan, because once Brad's father left the sparse windbreak provided by the stores and houses of the small farming community, visibility dropped down to zero feet. If it were up to Brad's father, who always joked that he did not inherit his Viking ancestors' sense of direction, he might easily have left the gravel road and headed the wrong way. Take it from a country boy, if you have never been out in the open prairie with a thirty-five to forty mile-per-hour wind driving heavy snow stinging and slicing into your face, you have no idea of the feeling of desperation and confusion that can overwhelm a person. The only thing he could see through the tiny slits in the scarf he had wrapped around his face to protect himself from the fierce wind and the freezing cold was a white sameness. The ditches at the side of the narrow gravel path had piled high with snow, which had swept across the road, making the route indistinguishable from the surrounding fields. In a few hours, the storm had disguised the familiar features of the countryside with mounds of snow.

And in less than an hour, it would be completely dark. There were no headlights on either old Dan or the small wagon. Finding their way home was about to accelerate very rapidly from Extremely Difficult to Nearly Impossible.

"Dan, old friend," Brad's father shouted above the howling wind, "it's up to you to get us home. I can't see a thing."

The moment he relaxed his hold on the reins, Old Dan seemed to understand. The first thing that the big draft horse did was turn around and head in the opposite direction.

He considered unhitching the wagon and getting on Dan's back, grabbing what supplies he could carry. But then he figured that as long as Dan stayed on the gravel road—and he seemed to know just where that was—the big fellow would be able to pull the small wagon without too much difficulty. Thankfully, he had not hitched up the dray wagon, but had chosen a smaller wagon, almost buggy size.

Dan was able to maintain a steady pace, and although Brad's mother was frantic with worry when his father and the powerful horse pulled up to the barn, the two hardy souls who had challenged the great snowstorm returned safely. Brad's mother helped rub Dan down with horse blankets, and they brought some extra straw for warm bedding for Dan and for Dolly, his stall companion. It is certain that Dan also received an extra helping or two of oats that night.

In later years when Brad's parents would tell the story of how Dan had found his way home in the snowstorm and after dark, Brad would ask just how *was* the horse able to navigate successfully under such adverse conditions.

His father would always shake his head and say that horses just have a way of being able to find their way home if the rider or driver surrenders the reins. "That's another reason why you must always treat a horse with respect and kindness and give it a good home," he would often add. "That way they'll always want to find their way back to their stall."

Brad feels that he was privileged to have witnessed the passing of an era on the Iowa farmstead. When he was a small boy, they still did a limited amount of farmwork using horses. They used the Farmall 20 and 12 tractors with the big iron wheels and the uncomfortable iron seats to do the plowing and other heavy field work, but the two horses, Dolly and Dan, were still very much in demand for a host of other duties.

Brad remembers that the job of pulling the corn, oats, and hay wagons was very much the province of the horses. His father used to signal them by making clicking noises with his tongue against his cheek whenever he wanted Dolly and Dan to move ahead a few feet, then stop. It seemed to Brad as a small boy that his father and the horses had some special kind of language that existed only between them. Uptown on Saturday nights in their small rural community, the children felt very cosmopolitan, because they heard adults speaking Norwegian at the north end of town, Danish in the middle, and German at the south end. But it seemed that his father and the horses had perfected yet another foreign tongue.

Click-click. Brad's father would make that peculiar sound, and the horses would walk ahead to the next fence post or the next shock of oats or corn and stop. Dolly and Dan would seem so confident, so self-assured that they understood exactly what he wanted them to do. Sometimes they would bend their necks down to the ground and their large, velvety muzzles would scoop some fallen kernels of corn or oats into their mouths. They would stand patiently, chewing the treat slowly, savoring the goodness, until the boss would sound the next *click-click.*

To a child's eyes, the two Belgian draft horses seemed like giants, and Brad was fascinated by the morning ritual of harnessing Dan and Dolly. From the placing of great collars with their shiny brass globes on their necks to the draping of the leather strips of fly-netting over their bodies, the entire process seemed to rival that of a knight preparing his charger for battle. And in a sense, his father was setting forth on a quest that would pit him against long, hard hours of field work with only Dolly and Dan at his side to aid him. Sometimes Brad's mom and he would walk out to the field where they were working, and Brad was always excited when they got to ride back in the wagon pulled by Dolly and Dan. In the hot, humid days of summer, the horses would return with flecks of lather streaking their bodies, and they would rub Dolly and Dan down with a couple old horse blankets and lead them to the cattle tank where they could take long drinks of cool water. In the twenty-below-zero days of winter, the breath of the hardworking animals would come out in great white clouds and ice particles would form on their collars. Sometimes back in their stalls, their backs would appear to be releasing steam when Brad's father removed the blankets from under their harness and reins.

Brad will always remember the affection and respect that his father showed toward Dolly and Dan. When Dolly passed away and Dan was too old to do any work, Brad's father retired him in the pasture to spend his last days roaming freely among the cattle.

Brad has a clear image of Dan standing at the far end of the pasture, his head lowered, seemingly lost in memories of days long past. Brad felt sorry for Dan, and some days he would bring the old fellow an apple from the orchard. His muzzle would take the treat gently from the boy's hands, and then Brad would see those large teeth, yellowed with age, grind away at that apple and dispatch it in a couple of gulps. Brad's mom didn't have to warn him twice to be careful when he handed Dan an apple. Brad could vividly imagine his little fingers between old Dan's chompers.

One day as Brad walked down their long lane after school, he looked to the west, where Dan always stood at the far end of the pasture. He wasn't there.

That night, as Brad helped his father with chores, he nodded and offered no details when Brad asked if Dan had died. Then, Brad walked away, leaving his father to silently mourn the old friend who had so stalwartly walked through a blinding blizzard to save his life.

$\mathcal{I}$n our book *Animal Miracles* (Adams Media 1999), Clarisa Bernhardt told of the time when she was twelve years old and was allowed to ride a beautiful—but independent-minded—quarter horse named Cinnamon across the pastures of Grandmother Loden's Texas farm. When they were far from the barn, Cinnamon protested the saddle that she deemed was too heavy by kneeling down near an irrigation ditch and refusing to move until her young rider removed it from her back.

As Clarisa was loosening the saddle, tugging at the reins, and trying to get Cinnamon out of the mud, the horse suddenly jumped to her feet and managed to toss off the heavy saddle so that it landed on her little mistress. Clarisa remembered that as she lay pinned under the saddle, she felt like crying, and she feared that Cinnamon would run back to the barn and leave her to drag the big saddle home by herself. Cinnamon trotted away in a self-satisfied trot, then turned to look at Clarisa lying sprawled in the mud as if to give her a horse laugh.

But Cinnamon did not run back to the barn and leave Clarisa to walk home alone. The horse suddenly snorted in alarm and began to run toward the little girl lying in the mud. As Clarisa watched in shock, Cinnamon approached a huge water moccasin that had slithered to within a few feet of her and had begun to coil and prepare to strike. The horse used its rear legs and hooves to kick the deadly snake high into the air so that it would land in the irrigation ditch far away from Clarisa. The horse with an attitude had saved Clarisa's life.

Clarisa told us that she would never forget that day when Cinnamon rose beyond her own fear and safety to save her. "The day Cinnamon saved my life," she said, "she acted on an inner awareness of the situation which awakened her ancient intuitive survival instincts and prompted them into quick action."

Since that day when she was a girl back in Texas, Clarisa has used her own intuitive talents to communicate with horses, humans, and other assorted beings thousands of times as she matured into a woman who has become famous for her telepathic and clairvoyant abilities. "Animals don't talk and speak words as humans do," Clarisa told us, "so the best way they can communicate is either telepathically by sending 'picture thoughts' or by speaking to someone in a dream. In my experience, they communicate quick thought forms that give the message precisely."

One winter when Clarisa was in Arizona, a friend asked if she could "talk" with his thoroughbred Astro Bravo. "I agreed to go to the racetrack when the horse was in training and we went to Astro Bravo's stall. I placed my hands on the horse's head as the owner held the halter to keep him still."

Clarisa received a telepathic message from Astro Bravo: "Change the iron bit the rider uses."

Clarisa "asked" the horse to explain, because the iron bit in a racehorse's mouth is standard. The slender iron bit goes inside the mouth and is attached to the long leather reins that the rider uses to guide and direct the horse. Astro Bravo did his best to explain that he wanted a bit that would be essentially made of leather.

"My friend was surprised," Clarisa said, "but as soon as he agreed to construct a bit from a combination of items which would include leather, Astro Bravo told me how he would run in the race on the following day. He would stay in the back for quite a long time, then he would challenge the two lead horses—and he would win."

The owner chuckled at this revelation. He told Clarisa that it was not Astro Bravo's style to hang back, but to charge ahead.

"The next day, Astro Bravo ran the race exactly as he had told me the evening before," Clarisa said. "I was thrilled and delighted—especially because Astro Bravo won."

Clarisa said that the thoroughbred Delphinus Star had been one of her particular favorites. She had even received a number of dream messages from him before she ever actually saw or met the horse. At this time she was living in Manitoba, Canada, and was married to a man who owned a number of racing horses.

"Delphinus Star had raced at Aqueduct and Delaware in the States, but had contracted a virus and nearly died," Clarisa said. "For months our partner kept him in Florida for treatment, but he was finally sent back to Winnipeg to our partner's farm. The veterinarian was not very encouraging, but I made a point of taking Delphinus Star lots of herbs, including red clover and echinacea. This new treatment started to work, so he began training again at our local track at Assiniblina Downs. Soon, he was entered in a race for the first time after his long period of convalescence."

The morning of the race, just as she was awakening, Clarisa received a telepathic message from Delphinus Star. "Here is exactly what it said," Clarisa told us: "'Everyone has been so good to me, and I am going to win the race today. I will get out from the starting gate and race ahead of all the other horses. They will not come near me. I will win.'"

Clarisa was so impressed by such a powerful and strong message that she relayed it to Delphinus Star's trainer, Patti R. "She laughed and told me that since this was Delphinus Star's first race since he had been off and ill for so long, this was just a tightener race for him," Clarisa recalled. "Patti told me not to expect too much of Delphinus Star. They had entered him in this race as another method of getting him in shape. There was no way that he was going to win."

To Clarisa's delight and everyone else's astonishment, Delphinus Star left the starting gate nicely and pulled out ahead of the others. "The other horses could not keep up with him," Clarisa said. "He won the race by many lengths, just as he had told me he would. It was a most exciting time. And I certainly reminded everyone that I had told them before the race exactly what Delphinus Star had said to me. That was a great communication."

Some years ago near Los Angeles, Clarisa was introduced to a lovely Belgian horse named Bernice, who had a career of allowing mentally handicapped children to ride safely on her. "Bernice was one of a wonderful group of horses who had such an important responsibility, but I was particularly attracted to her," Clarisa said, "so I walked up to her and placed my hands on her head and asked her if she was having a nice day."

Clarisa received a happy telepathic response in reply to her question: "Yes, a nice little girl gave me some strawberries and I also got a carrot. But I liked the strawberry best."

Clarisa laughed and repeated what Bernice had said. The instructor became a little flustered, and said that a little girl had brought a pack of strawberries and shared them with Bernice. Someone else had given the horse a carrot. But how could Clarisa know?

"Bernice told me," Clarisa quietly answered.

When we asked Clarisa Bernhardt if she had any advice for those who might wish to communicate with their horse or animal friend, she provided these tips:

"If you wish to try such communication, just hold a picture-thought in your mind and see very clearly a picture of the commands you want your horse to do. For example, if you want the horse to come to you, mentally/telepathically say, 'Come here.' Next visualize the horse walking toward you. Then clear your thought forms and allow the action to occur. You can also ask a telepathic question of your horse. As you carefully and gently place your hands on its face or forehead, mentally ask the question. You'll be surprised at the responses you can quickly receive. Always remember to move your hands slowly so as not to frighten or startle your horse. Try it—and have fun!"

*I*t has been a long-held and widespread belief that animals could not possibly experience emotion. In fact if anyone were to express an opinion to the contrary, he or she would be considered a heretic to common reason and science.

Horses are *herd* animals, who in the wild rarely pair off with one another. Characteristically, it has been believed they are incapable of forming lasting bonds. More recently, however, it has been observed that domesticated horses who are paired off and share the same enclosed living quarters may not only develop feelings for one another, but may forge a lifetime bond—one that might be deeper than we could know.

In their bestselling book, *When Elephants Weep* (Delacorte Press, Bantam Doubleday Dell Publishing Group, Inc.: New York, 1995), Jeffrey Moussaieff

Masson and Susan McCarthy present a bold thesis backed with convincing evidence that animals do indeed possess emotions. Among the many fascinating cases cited is an account of two horses who exhibited a strong emotional bond with one another, something not deemed typical.

Masson and McCarthy recount a touching story of Alle and Ackman, two circus horses who were stabled together. Nobody in the circus noticed anything unusual about the horses—in either their individual behavior or their shared reactions to one another. There was absolutely no display of affection or attachment, until, that is, Ackman's sudden and unexpected death.

Alle became inconsolable, barely eating, hardly sleeping, and continually vocalizing discontent. Even though Alle grew weaker, the constant whinnying or neighing did not cease. Special tests and examinations were given to determine if Alle was sick. When no illness was found, to be on the safe side, medication was administered to keep up the horse's strength and urge it toward recovery from *whatever* was ailing it.

In hope of distracting and redirecting Alle's mysterious behavior, attempts were made by the circus staff to bolster the horse's spirits and resolve the crisis in every imaginable manner. Alle was moved in with other horses, given special food, attention, and treats. Nothing, not even other equine companionship, seemed to help. Within months, as Alle continued to pine, the horse wasted away and died of what was believed to be a lonely, broken, and grieving heart.

Grieving over the loss of a companion in human nature is considered an expression of love. Why should we think it would be different for an animal such as a horse like Alle?

Pride is an emotion. Secretariat, the famous racehorse, seemed to exhibit a sense of himself and his own particular style of running. Although many often referred to Secretariat as ornery, temperamental, and stubborn, it was most likely that it was a proper understanding of this horse's sensitivity that led to his huge success. Secretariat soared to international fame when he was a Triple Crown winner of the Kentucky Derby, the Preakness, and the Belmont Stakes races in 1973.

This normally docile horse would absolutely refuse to run unless he did it his way! Rather than attempting to make him conform to an accepted winning strategy—or give up on him altogether—Secretariat's trainers and jockeys allowed him the sense of pride to run a race in his own way. It was Secretariat's unusual burst of speed either at the beginning or at the end of the race that came to be his trademarked winning style.

It was often noted, upon winning, no matter how exhausted, hot, and thirsty the magnificent horse was, he would lift his head high, stick out his chest, and pose in a manner fitting of his dignity, as if to proudly say, "I did it my way!"

*L*ouis Sanchez, a farmer from Oklahoma, is convinced horses are very intelligent beings with feelings similar to those that humans experience. "Fear, pride, sadness, joy, grief—horses feel these things, too. Not only in interaction with humans, but also with each other," Louis exclaimed. "I've seen it with my own eyes!"

To illustrate his beliefs, Louis told us of the following incident that occurred on his farm several harvests ago. A particularly abundant year for his corn crop, Louis had been out in the fields of his 400-plus-acre farm, harvesting row after row. It was time to give the corn picker a slight rest and empty the wagons that were overflowing with corn kernels. Louis would take some loads to the elevator in town and some to his own bins on the farm, readying them for the next round of picking.

Confessing that he still used what many farmers considered antiques, he told us that he favored the use of his trusty old 1961 IHC Farmall 240 utility tractor for hauling the wagons. He felt the old tractors worked just as well or better, because they didn't cost an arm and a leg.

Louis was enjoying the distinct autumn smells; the aroma of harvest; the mild, comfortable temperatures of the late September, mid-afternoon sun—his favorite time of the year. Sitting high up on his old tractor with the sun at his back, Louis felt pride and thankfulness as he surveyed the land. In all directions, stretching over miles and miles, as far as the eye could see, was soil tendered by the sweat of his ancestors. Blessed to have inherited the knowledge and skills, as well as the acres from his father and grandfather who'd farmed it before him, he couldn't fathom doing anything other than this. Farming was a perfect lifestyle, and he loved every minute of it.

Still somewhat in reverie, Louis continued: "While on the way to the elevator in town, something caught my attention."

Looking over his shoulder as he passed the pasture where his two horses, Taco and Tabasco, often grazed, a flash of frenzied activity stood out in stark contrast to the serenity and stillness of the surrounding fields.

"It was Taco, my colt. And I couldn't for the life of me figure out why he was acting so strangely," Louis said.

Taco was rearing up on his hind legs, jumping, and running back and forth toward Louis, then back the opposite direction, repeating these actions while snorting and neighing loudly.

"The grazing field covered a vast area, dotted with pockets of trees, hills, and valleys and striped with a little creek that ran through it," Louis said. "I knew there were many places where Tabasco, the filly, could be out of sight, but I thought that the way Taco was acting, I should go investigate. Taco was making the signs of a horse in trouble."

Louis proceeded down the dusty gravel road until he reached a point where he could change directions and head back toward his barn. Overflowing wagon attached, Louis said he tried to pick up a little speed, until the haste was only making waste and every bump was spilling out dribbles of corn.

Just short of the barn door and barely getting the tractor and wagon stopped, Louis turned off the engine of the tractor, hobbled off as fast as his arthritic knees would allow, and headed toward his old black Ford pickup. The key was always left in the ignition, "So she's ready to go," Louis boasted. "I figured I needed to find out mighty quick what was ailing that horse, and I didn't want to take the time to run in the house to get Ma or call George, our vet. I just flew over the bumpy dirt road in my pickup."

When Louis pulled into one of the gullies along the pasture, a particular spot he knew he hadn't yet had the time to repair, he could barely see through the dust cloud he'd made on the road, but he leaped out after opening the squeaky truck door. He knew he could make it through the barbed-wire fence fairly easy at that location, but he would have to walk a bit to get to the spot where he'd seen his Taco jumping around so peculiarly.

"Taco either heard the roar of the old pickup, knew I was coming, saw me, or sensed me," Louis said, "because he got to me first."

Uncertain still as to what was behind these strange goings-on, Louis didn't know what he could do to calm down his horse, which was acting wilder than any bucking bronco he'd ever seen—even at a rodeo. Taco was jumping around so frantically, Louis was afraid that if he attempted to approach the horse, he might be kicked or trampled in the process.

"As soon as Taco got close enough to me to be certain I was paying attention to him," Louis said, "he'd run the other direction for a distance, then stop and wait for me to catch up."

Louis finally figured out that Taco was trying to lead him somewhere to Tabasco. There must be something wrong with his buddy. Taco's game plan stayed the same. He would race ahead, bucking, whinnying, snorting; then he'd stop and wait until Louis reached that spot.

"Hobbling along on my old arthritic knees, I was so out of breath, I didn't think I would be able to go much farther without resting," Louis grumbled. "That doggone horse wouldn't let me stop, just kept rearing up at me to keep going."

Finally, as they approached a fairly deep ditch, down by the creek bed, Taco came to a halting stop. Although still neighing, snorting, and breathing hard and fast, Taco stopped bucking and suddenly exhibited a calm manner. He was assured that help was on its way, as he remained there, waiting for Louis to catch up.

Taco became still as a fence post and stood sentry over something that Louis couldn't see until he climbed the rest of the hill.

"By the time I reached Taco, I was panting and snorting louder than he was," Louis said. "I thought I was having a heart attack—right there on the spot, and I never would find out what was so doggone important."

The shock of seeing his other horse, Tabasco, piled in a heap at the bottom of a deep gully snapped

Louis's heart back into normal sinus rhythm and back to reality.

"Calling out her name as I clumsily tumbled down the hill to get to her, I didn't know if she was even alive," Louis said sadly. "Then I could see that she had broken a leg when she had stumbled and fallen to the bottom of the gully. Finally, she heard me and started to whinny as if asking me for help. I knelt beside her and stroked her head and neck, so happy that she was still alive."

Then, like a bolt of lightning, Taco took off, leaving both Tabasco and Louis there at the bottom of the semi-dried-up creek bed in the ravine.

At that point in his narrative, Louis said that he'd have to digress slightly before the rest of the story would make sense. Once a year for fifteen years, Louis and the rest of his family had taken part in a historic little festival called Heritage Days, where the old ways of farming were demonstrated. Side by side, their wonderful horses, Taco and Tabasco, were hitched to wagons that they would pull, as in days gone by. Eager little children and adults alike would go for hayrides that these horses seemed to be proud to lead.

"It was an event that I swear the horses looked forward to and enjoyed as much as, if not more, than the rest of us," Louis explained. "Whether Taco made the association or not, I cannot prove, but it was in no time that he was back, standing at the top of the ravine with a rope in his mouth that he had taken from a peg near his stall, shaking his head from side to side. It was as if he was saying, 'Use the rope to pull Tabasco out of the ravine.'"

With what must have been some kind of understanding or thought about how ropes could be used to save his friend, Taco seemed to know that Louis would now somehow be able to help Tabasco. Taco had raced to the barn and returned with a tool for the rescue.

"I knew Taco's plan immediately," Louis said. "I looped the rope around Tabasco's upper body and shoulders, being careful to avoid creating a pull on her broken back leg. Then I tied the other end of the rope around Taco's strong neck. Together, we were able to pull Tabasco until she stood upright and was able to limp up out of the ravine."

Louis added that in the old days, a horse with a broken leg would probably have been put down, but there was no way that he could prescribe such a fate for his beloved filly. Louis called George, their veterinarian, who bandaged Tabasco's break and placed a brace on it.

"The whole family—and especially Taco—gave Tabasco plenty of tender loving care until she was able to leave the stall and walk on her leg," Louis concluded.

*B*ack in the autumn of 1968, Philip Clay was a no-nonsense traffic policeman who had proved more than once while on duty to have nerves of steel. Clay said that in those days he prided himself on not being afraid of anything. But then came the night when he distinctly saw a group of ghostly horseback riders on a lonely stretch of A640 outside of Huddersfield, England.

Officer Clay was driving home at 1:30 A.M. after completing an evening shift when he saw the phantom highwaymen coming toward him. There were two riders dressed in seventeenth-century attire, with velvet coats, hats, boots, pistols, and swords. A third rider was clad in peasant attire and was leading a packhorse.

Clay couldn't believe his eyes. He circled his automobile and drove past them again. They were still there. Four horses and three riders dressed in period costumes of the seventeenth century. In a corner of his mind, Officer Clay was concluding that the riders and their steeds had to be ghosts, but he told Jenny Parkin of *The Huddersfield Daily Examiner* (September 15, 2003) that the figures were absolutely lifelike and not at all transparent. They were quite solid highwaymen on quite solid horses.

The policeman, who had seen some pretty gory sights in his day—but nothing to match a bunch of ghost riders—turned around yet a third time to convince himself completely that the phantoms were, indeed, there on the A640.

But on this occasion, as Officer Clay slowed his car and was about to stop, one of the riders acknowledged his presence by raising his hand, touching the brim of his hat, and bowing. That was when, Clay admitted, he lost his nerve and drove away.

In the days following his sighting of the ghostly figures, Officer Clay tried to find out if there had been some sort of fancy-dress ball going on in the area or if there might had been some charity event requiring the participants to dress in seventeenth-century costume. In spite of his persistent quest to find a logical explanation for the phantom highwaymen, the policeman found none. However, while researching the mysterious event, he was told by some individuals that ghosts were often sighted in the very Buckstones area in which he had seen the apparitions. Thirty-five years later, Clay, now seventy-four and retired, is still baffled by the encounter.

*T*hroughout this book, we have shared stories in which people have expressed their belief that horses have communicated with them, empathized with them when they were happy or sad, sympathized with them to the point of shedding tears, and even rescued them. These people all believe beyond a shadow of a doubt that horses have feelings and are able to recognize the love of owner, caregiver, or enthusiast, reciprocating accordingly and exceeding any preconceived thoughts or expectations or old scientific notions.

We are reminded again that we have been put here on this planet in a web of life more intricate and interconnected than most of us heretofore have realized. Perhaps humans aren't the only ones who have been gifted with the ability to think, reason, feel, and show emotions. We are but caretakers who need to wake up and listen to the voice of our brother and sister four-leggeds, the regal horses.

Perhaps horses have much to teach us about life—and about *miracles* if we but listen.